Operation Anaconda: The 2002 U.S. Military Operation in Eastern Afghanistan

Table of Contents

Operation Anaconda: The 2002 U.S. Military Operation in Eastern Afghanistan

By Roberto Miguel Rodriguez

Chapter 1: Operation Anaconda: The 2002 U.S. Military Operation in Eastern Afghanistan

Background and Context of Operation Anaconda

Operation Anaconda: The Untold Story of the 2002 U.S. Military Operation in Eastern Afghanistan

Introduction:

Operation Anaconda, which took place in early 2002, was a significant military operation conducted by the United States in eastern Afghanistan. This subchapter aims to provide historians and specialists in various niches related to Operation Anaconda with an in-depth understanding of the background and context of this operation.

1. Operation Anaconda: The 2002 U.S. Military Operation in Eastern Afghanistan:

Operation Anaconda was a joint military operation involving U.S. Army, Navy, Air Force, and Marine Corps, supported by coalition forces. It aimed to root out and eliminate Taliban and Al-Qaeda forces in the rugged mountains of eastern Afghanistan.

2. Special Forces Operations During Operation Anaconda:

Special forces played a crucial role in Operation Anaconda, conducting reconnaissance, intelligence gathering, and engaging in direct combat with enemy forces. Their expertise and unique capabilities were instrumental in achieving mission objectives.

3. Air Support Strategies Used in Operation Anaconda:

The success of Operation Anaconda heavily relied on effective air support strategies. Close air support, precision airstrikes, and helicopter insertion and extraction were employed to provide cover, suppress enemy forces, and transport troops and supplies.

4. Intelligence Gathering Techniques Employed During Operation Anaconda:

Intelligence gathering played a vital role in Operation Anaconda, with a focus on locating and neutralizing enemy forces. Techniques such as signals intelligence, human intelligence, and aerial surveillance were utilized to gather actionable intelligence.

5. Role of Local Afghan Militias in Supporting Operation Anaconda:

Local Afghan militias, known as Afghan National Army and Afghan Local Police, played a significant role in supporting Operation Anaconda. They provided critical intelligence, acted as guides in the rough terrain, and fought alongside U.S. and coalition forces.

6. Medical Evacuation and Field Hospital Operations During Operation Anaconda:

The challenging mountainous terrain and intense combat operations necessitated efficient medical evacuation and field hospital operations. The medical teams worked tirelessly to evacuate and treat wounded personnel, saving countless lives.

7. Analysis of the Command and Control Structure in Operation Anaconda:

A detailed analysis of the command and control structure during Operation Anaconda provides insights into the decision-making processes, coordination among various units, and the effectiveness of the military leadership.

8. Use of Advanced Weaponry and Technology in Operation Anaconda:

Operation Anaconda witnessed the utilization of advanced weaponry and technology, including precision-guided munitions, unmanned aerial vehicles, and night vision equipment. These assets provided a significant advantage to the U.S. and coalition forces.

9. Psychological Operations and Information Warfare in Operation Anaconda:

Psychological operations and information warfare played a crucial role in shaping the operational environment and influencing the local population. Propaganda dissemination and psychological tactics were employed to gain support and undermine the enemy's morale.

10. Humanitarian Assistance Efforts During Operation Anaconda:

Despite being a military operation, Operation Anaconda also included humanitarian assistance efforts. These efforts aimed to win the hearts and minds of the local population by providing medical aid, food, and infrastructure support.

11. Lessons Learned and Strategic Implications of Operation Anaconda for Future Military Operations in Afghanistan:

A thorough analysis of Operation Anaconda's outcomes and lessons learned provides valuable insights for future military operations in Afghanistan. This section highlights strategic implications, tactical adjustments, and recommendations for future missions.

Conclusion:

Understanding the background and context of Operation Anaconda is crucial for historians and specialists studying this significant military operation. This subchapter provides a comprehensive overview of the operation, covering various niches related to Operation Anaconda.

Objectives and Planning of Operation Anaconda

Operation Anaconda was a crucial military operation conducted by the United States in Eastern Afghanistan in 2002. This subchapter aims to provide historians and enthusiasts of Operation Anaconda with an in-depth understanding of the operation's objectives and planning.

The primary objective of Operation Anaconda was to eliminate Al-Qaeda and Taliban forces that had taken refuge in the Shahikot Valley. This area had become a significant stronghold for these terrorist groups, posing a significant threat to regional stability and the ongoing efforts to stabilize Afghanistan. The operation aimed to disrupt their operational capabilities and deny them safe havens.

Extensive planning was carried out to ensure the success of Operation Anaconda. The operation involved a coordinated effort between the U.S. military, Afghan security forces, and local Afghan militias. The planning phase focused on developing a comprehensive strategy that incorporated special forces operations, air support strategies, intelligence gathering techniques, and the utilization of advanced weaponry and technology.

Special forces played a crucial role in Operation Anaconda, conducting direct action missions, reconnaissance, and intelligence gathering. Their expertise and training were instrumental in identifying enemy positions and providing real-time intelligence to the overall command structure.

Air support played a vital role in Operation Anaconda, with a focus on precision strikes and close air support to provide cover for ground forces. The planning phase involved determining the most effective air support strategies to minimize civilian casualties while maximizing the damage inflicted on enemy forces.

Intelligence gathering techniques employed during Operation Anaconda were diverse and extensive. This included the use of advanced surveillance technology, human intelligence sources, and signals intelligence to gather critical information about enemy movements, capabilities, and intentions.

The role of local Afghan militias cannot be overstated. These militias played a crucial role in supporting Operation Anaconda by providing valuable local knowledge, acting as guides in the treacherous terrain, and assisting in the identification and neutralization of enemy forces.

To ensure the success of Operation Anaconda, medical evacuation and field hospital operations were meticulously planned. The provision of immediate medical care to wounded personnel was essential in maintaining the morale and effectiveness of the fighting force.

The command and control structure in Operation Anaconda was analyzed and refined to ensure effective coordination between different units and agencies involved. This helped facilitate timely decision-making and the rapid deployment of forces.

Operation Anaconda also witnessed the use of advanced weaponry and technology. This included precision-guided munitions, unmanned aerial vehicles, and advanced communication systems, all of which significantly enhanced the operational capabilities of the U.S. forces.

Psychological operations and information warfare played a critical role in Operation Anaconda. Efforts were made to undermine enemy morale, disrupt their communication networks, and counter their propaganda efforts, thereby creating an advantageous psychological environment for the U.S. forces.

Despite the primary focus being on military objectives, Operation Anaconda also included humanitarian assistance efforts. These efforts aimed to win the hearts and minds of the local population, providing support in areas such as healthcare, education, and infrastructure development.

Finally, Operation Anaconda provided valuable lessons and strategic implications for future military operations in Afghanistan. The analysis of the operation's successes and challenges helped shape future strategies, tactics, and decision-making processes, as well as emphasizing the importance of comprehensive planning and coordination.

In conclusion, Operation Anaconda was a complex military operation with multiple objectives and meticulous planning. The combined efforts of special forces, air support, intelligence gathering, local Afghan militias, medical evacuation operations, advanced technology, psychological operations, information warfare, and humanitarian assistance contributed to the overall success of the operation. The lessons learned from Operation Anaconda continue to shape future military operations in Afghanistan.

Deployment and Initial Phase of Operation Anaconda

The deployment and initial phase of Operation Anaconda marked a critical turning point in the 2002 U.S. military operation in Eastern Afghanistan. Historians have extensively studied this phase, as it set the stage for the intense combat that followed. This subchapter explores the various aspects of the deployment and initial phase of Operation Anaconda, shedding light on the strategies and techniques employed by the U.S. military.

The Special Forces operations during Operation Anaconda were characterized by their exceptional skill and bravery. These elite units played a crucial role in gathering intelligence, conducting reconnaissance, and engaging with enemy forces. Their expertise in unconventional warfare proved invaluable in the challenging terrain of the Shah-i-Kot Valley.

Air support strategies were a key component of Operation Anaconda. The U.S. military employed a variety of aircraft, including attack helicopters, fighter jets, and unmanned aerial vehicles, to provide close air support to ground forces. The effective coordination between ground and air units ensured the success of numerous combat operations and minimized casualties.

Intelligence gathering techniques used during Operation Anaconda were instrumental in identifying enemy positions and intentions. Advanced surveillance technology, human intelligence sources, and signals intelligence played vital roles in providing real-time information to commanders. This intelligence allowed for informed decision-making and enabled the U.S. military to maintain the initiative throughout the operation.

Local Afghan militias played a significant role in supporting Operation Anaconda. These militias, trained and equipped by the U.S. military, provided valuable assistance in securing key areas, conducting patrols, and gathering intelligence. Their knowledge of the local terrain and cultural dynamics proved invaluable in the success of the operation.

Medical evacuation and field hospital operations during Operation Anaconda were critical in providing timely medical care to wounded soldiers. The establishment of forward operating bases and the deployment of medical personnel and resources ensured that injured personnel received immediate attention, increasing their chances of survival.

The command and control structure in Operation Anaconda was meticulously organized and executed. The integration of various military units, including Special Forces, conventional forces, and coalition partners, required effective coordination and communication. The command structure ensured unity of effort and facilitated the rapid adaptation of strategies based on changing battlefield conditions.

Advanced weaponry and technology played a pivotal role in Operation Anaconda. The use of precision-guided munitions, night vision devices, and cutting-edge communication systems enhanced the effectiveness and lethality of U.S. forces. The operational tempo and combat power displayed by the U.S. military showcased the advancements made in military technology.

Psychological operations and information warfare were employed to undermine the enemy's morale and disrupt their command and control capabilities. Through leaflet drops, radio broadcasts, and cyber warfare tactics, the U.S. military aimed to shape the battlefield narrative and erode the enemy's will to fight.

Humanitarian assistance efforts during Operation Anaconda showcased the U.S. military's commitment to the Afghan people. Medical outreach programs, infrastructure development projects, and the provision of basic necessities aimed to win the hearts and minds of the local population and create a favorable environment for stability and security.

The lessons learned from Operation Anaconda have significant strategic implications for future military operations in Afghanistan. The operation highlighted the importance of intelligence, coordination, and adaptability. It underscored the need for a comprehensive approach that combines military, political, and humanitarian efforts to achieve long-term success in counterinsurgency operations.

In conclusion, the deployment and initial phase of Operation Anaconda set the stage for the intense combat that followed in the Shah-i-Kot Valley. The strategies, techniques, and lessons learned from this phase provide invaluable insights for historians studying Operation Anaconda and shed light on the complexities of modern military operations in Afghanistan.

Challenges and Obstacles Faced by U.S. Forces in Eastern Afghanistan

In the subchapter titled "Challenges and Obstacles Faced by U.S. Forces in Eastern Afghanistan," we delve into the arduous journey of Operation Anaconda, the 2002 U.S. military operation in Eastern Afghanistan. This section aims to provide historians with a comprehensive understanding of the difficulties encountered by U.S. forces during this multifaceted campaign.

As the operation unfolded, U.S. forces faced a myriad of challenges unique to the rugged terrain and complex geopolitical dynamics of Eastern Afghanistan. The inhospitable environment, characterized by steep mountains and dense vegetation, posed significant obstacles to both maneuverability and communication. Special forces operating in this region had to adapt their strategies to contend with these physical barriers, relying on their extensive training and experience in unconventional warfare.

To ensure the success of Operation Anaconda, U.S. forces relied heavily on air support strategies. However, the mountainous terrain presented challenges for aerial operations, including limited visibility and the risk of friendly fire incidents. This subchapter explores the innovative tactics employed by U.S. pilots and the use of advanced technologies to mitigate these challenges, ultimately enabling effective air support throughout the operation.

Intelligence gathering played a pivotal role in Operation Anaconda. This subchapter examines the sophisticated techniques employed by U.S. forces to gather critical information, including satellite imagery, signals intelligence, and human intelligence. By leveraging these methods, U.S. forces were able to gain valuable insights into enemy positions and intentions, enabling them to plan and execute successful operations.

Local Afghan militias also played a significant role in supporting Operation Anaconda. This subchapter explores the complexities of working with these groups, their motivations, and the challenges faced in coordinating efforts between U.S. forces and Afghan militias. The collaboration between U.S. forces and local allies highlights the importance of building relationships and fostering trust in counterinsurgency operations.

Additionally, this subchapter delves into the intricate operations of medical evacuation and field hospitals during Operation Anaconda. It examines the challenges faced by medical personnel in providing life-saving care in a hostile environment, highlighting the agility and resilience of the U.S. medical teams.

Furthermore, the analysis of the command and control structure in Operation Anaconda sheds light on the decision-making processes and coordination between various military units. The use of advanced weaponry and technology is explored, showcasing how these capabilities enhanced the effectiveness of U.S. forces in the operation.

Psychological operations and information warfare were integral to Operation Anaconda. This subchapter analyzes the strategies employed to shape the perception of the local population and disrupt enemy communication networks, ultimately contributing to the success of the mission.

Lastly, this subchapter examines the humanitarian assistance efforts during Operation Anaconda, emphasizing the U.S. military's commitment to providing aid and support to the Afghan population affected by the conflict.

By thoroughly analyzing the challenges and obstacles faced by U.S. forces in Eastern Afghanistan during Operation Anaconda, historians gain invaluable insights into the complexities of modern warfare. The lessons learned and strategic implications derived from this operation will serve as a guide for future military operations in Afghanistan, ensuring the continued improvement and effectiveness of U.S. military endeavors in this region.

Overall Assessment of Operation Anaconda's Success

The 2002 U.S. Military Operation in Eastern Afghanistan, known as Operation Anaconda, was a complex and challenging military operation aimed at eliminating Taliban and Al-Qaeda forces from the region. In this subchapter, we will provide an overall assessment of the operation's success, considering various aspects such as special forces operations, air support strategies, intelligence gathering techniques, the role of local Afghan militias, medical evacuation and field hospital operations, command and control structure, advanced weaponry and technology, psychological operations and information warfare, humanitarian assistance efforts, and the strategic implications and lessons learned for future military operations in Afghanistan.

Operation Anaconda can be considered a success in many respects. Special forces played a crucial role in carrying out reconnaissance and direct action missions, targeting high-value enemy personnel and capturing crucial intelligence. Their operations were instrumental in disrupting enemy networks and weakening their overall capabilities.

Air support played a pivotal role in Operation Anaconda. The use of precision airstrikes, close air support, and aerial surveillance greatly assisted ground forces in identifying and neutralizing enemy positions. The successful coordination between ground and air forces ensured minimal collateral damage and maximized the operational effectiveness of the mission.

Intelligence gathering techniques employed during Operation Anaconda were comprehensive and effective. The integration of human intelligence, signals intelligence, and satellite imagery provided commanders with real-time situational awareness, enabling them to make informed decisions and adapt their strategies accordingly.

Local Afghan militias played a significant role in supporting Operation Anaconda. Their knowledge of the terrain, language, and cultural dynamics proved invaluable in gathering intelligence and providing support to U.S. forces. Their participation helped bridge the gap between the local population and the coalition forces, enhancing the overall effectiveness of the operation.

Medical evacuation and field hospital operations were critical in saving the lives of wounded soldiers. The rapid response and efficient medical care provided by the military medical personnel ensured that casualties were minimized and soldiers received the necessary treatment to recover and return to duty.

The command and control structure in Operation Anaconda demonstrated effective coordination and communication among various units and agencies involved. The establishment of a unified command structure facilitated the seamless integration of efforts and resources, resulting in a well-coordinated and synchronized operation.

The use of advanced weaponry and technology enhanced the operational capabilities of U.S. forces during Operation Anaconda. Precision-guided munitions, unmanned aerial vehicles, and advanced surveillance systems provided a significant advantage, allowing for precise targeting and minimizing the risks to coalition forces.

Psychological operations and information warfare played an essential role in shaping the narrative and countering enemy propaganda. The dissemination of accurate information, combined with targeted psychological operations, helped to win the hearts and minds of the local population and isolate the enemy further.

Humanitarian assistance efforts during Operation Anaconda were crucial in building trust and fostering goodwill among the local population. The provision of medical aid, infrastructure development, and support for education and economic development helped to improve the lives of the Afghan people, creating a stable environment for long-term peace and security.

Operation Anaconda provided numerous lessons learned and strategic implications for future military operations in Afghanistan. It highlighted the importance of comprehensive intelligence gathering, the integration of special forces and local militias, the effective use of air support, and the need for a well-coordinated command and control structure. Additionally, the operation emphasized the significance of psychological operations, humanitarian assistance, and the use of advanced technology in achieving operational success.

In conclusion, Operation Anaconda can be considered a success on multiple fronts. Its comprehensive approach, effective utilization of resources, and successful coordination among various elements contributed to the weakening of Taliban and Al-Qaeda forces in the region. The operation provided valuable insights and strategic implications for future military operations in Afghanistan, ensuring that the lessons learned are applied to enhance the effectiveness and efficiency of future endeavors in the region.

Chapter 2: Special Forces Operations during Operation Anaconda

Role and Importance of Special Forces in Operation Anaconda

In the context of Operation Anaconda, the role and importance of Special Forces cannot be overstated. These elite units played a crucial part in the success of the operation, showcasing their unique skills, training, and capabilities. This subchapter will delve into the pivotal contribution of Special Forces during Operation Anaconda, highlighting their diverse roles and highlighting their importance in achieving the mission's objectives.

Special Forces operations during Operation Anaconda were characterized by their versatility and adaptability. These highly trained soldiers were at the forefront of the battle, carrying out a range of tasks such as reconnaissance, direct action, and unconventional warfare. They operated deep behind enemy lines, gathering critical intelligence, conducting raids on enemy positions, and disrupting enemy supply lines. Their ability to operate in hostile and rugged terrain, often under extreme conditions, proved instrumental in gaining a tactical advantage over the enemy.

Air support strategies used in Operation Anaconda were closely integrated with Special Forces operations. Special Forces liaised with air assets, including helicopters and close air support aircraft, to provide precision strikes on enemy positions. This coordination allowed for swift and targeted engagements, minimizing the risk to friendly forces and maximizing the impact on the enemy.

Intelligence gathering techniques employed during Operation Anaconda were enhanced by Special Forces units. These highly skilled operatives utilized their expertise in human intelligence, signals intelligence, and imagery intelligence to collect actionable information. Special Forces teams worked closely with local Afghan militias, building relationships and leveraging their knowledge of the terrain and local population to gain valuable insights into enemy activities.

The role of local Afghan militias in supporting Operation Anaconda should not be underestimated. These militias, often referred to as Afghan National Army and Afghan Northern Alliance forces, fought alongside the U.S. military and Special Forces, providing critical support and local knowledge. Their familiarity with the region and their ability to navigate the complex tribal dynamics proved invaluable in the success of the operation.

Medical evacuation and field hospital operations during Operation Anaconda were a critical aspect of the mission. Special Forces medical personnel played a vital role in providing immediate care to wounded soldiers, often under fire. Their expertise in trauma medicine and their ability to stabilize and evacuate casualties significantly contributed to the survival rate of wounded personnel.

The command and control structure in Operation Anaconda showcased the seamless integration of Special Forces units with conventional forces. Special Forces teams provided real-time intelligence, advising senior commanders and shaping the overall strategy. Their ability to operate independently and adapt to rapidly changing situations ensured effective coordination and the swift execution of operational plans.

Advanced weaponry and technology were extensively utilized during Operation Anaconda, giving Special Forces a significant advantage over the enemy. From cutting-edge night vision goggles to precision-guided munitions, these resources enhanced their capabilities and allowed for precise and effective engagements.

Psychological operations and information warfare were key components of Operation Anaconda. Special Forces units played a vital role in disseminating information, shaping the narrative, and undermining enemy morale. Their expertise in psychological operations contributed to the success of the mission by influencing the perception of the enemy and winning the hearts and minds of the local population.

Humanitarian assistance efforts during Operation Anaconda demonstrated the broader strategic objectives of the operation. Special Forces units worked closely with local communities, providing aid and support to win their trust and cooperation. These efforts helped to build a positive relationship between the U.S. military and the Afghan people, contributing to the long-term stability of the region.

In conclusion, the role and importance of Special Forces in Operation Anaconda cannot be overstated. From their diverse range of operations to their integration with conventional forces, these elite units were instrumental in achieving the mission's objectives. The success of Operation Anaconda serves as a testament to the invaluable contribution of Special Forces and offers valuable lessons for future military operations in Afghanistan.

Special Forces Tactics and Strategies Utilized in Eastern Afghanistan

During Operation Anaconda, the Special Forces played a critical role in the success of the 2002 U.S. military operation in Eastern Afghanistan. This subchapter explores the tactics and strategies employed by these elite units, shedding light on their contributions to the overall mission.

One of the key tactics utilized by Special Forces during Operation Anaconda was the concept of "force multiplication." By training and working closely with local Afghan militias, the Special Forces were able to leverage their knowledge of the terrain, culture, and language to gain a significant advantage. These partnerships allowed for better intelligence gathering, improved situational awareness, and enhanced operational effectiveness.

In terms of tactics, the Special Forces employed a wide range of techniques. They utilized unconventional warfare tactics, including guerrilla warfare and hit-and-run tactics, to disrupt enemy movements and weaken their positions. These tactics were effective in countering the Taliban's traditional warfare strategies, providing a significant advantage to the U.S. forces.

Another critical aspect of the Special Forces' strategy was the use of advanced weaponry and technology. They leveraged cutting-edge equipment, such as drones and surveillance systems, to gather intelligence and conduct reconnaissance. By utilizing these tools, they were able to identify enemy positions, monitor their movements, and provide real-time information to the command center.

The Special Forces also played a crucial role in the command and control structure of Operation Anaconda. Their expertise in small unit tactics and decentralized command allowed for more efficient decision-making and rapid response to changing situations. This flexibility was essential in the dynamic and unpredictable terrain of Eastern Afghanistan.

Psychological operations and information warfare were other key components of the Special Forces' strategy. They utilized propaganda, leaflet drops, and radio broadcasts to demoralize the enemy and win the hearts and minds of the local population. This approach helped to undermine the Taliban's influence and gain support from the Afghan people.

Furthermore, the Special Forces played a significant role in the humanitarian assistance efforts during Operation Anaconda. They provided medical evacuation and operated field hospitals, ensuring the well-being of both U.S. forces and local civilians caught in the crossfire.

These efforts not only saved lives but also helped to build trust and support from the Afghan population.

In conclusion, the Special Forces' tactics and strategies were instrumental in the success of Operation Anaconda in Eastern Afghanistan. Their ability to adapt to the local environment, utilize advanced technology, and forge alliances with local Afghan militias proved to be a winning formula. The lessons learned from this operation have strategic implications for future military operations in Afghanistan, emphasizing the importance of leveraging local partnerships, employing advanced weaponry, and integrating psychological operations and humanitarian assistance efforts.

Covert Operations and Infiltration Techniques Used by Special Forces

In the subchapter "Covert Operations and Infiltration Techniques Used by Special Forces," we delve into the secretive and strategic methods employed by the U.S. Special Forces during Operation Anaconda in Eastern Afghanistan in 2002. This chapter aims to provide a comprehensive understanding of the tactics and strategies used by these elite units to achieve their objectives while operating behind enemy lines.

Special Forces operations during Operation Anaconda were characterized by their clandestine nature. Our historical analysis reveals that these highly trained soldiers executed covert missions with precision and finesse, infiltrating enemy territory undetected. Utilizing their expertise in unconventional warfare, they employed various infiltration techniques such as HALO (High Altitude Low Opening) and HAHO (High Altitude High Opening) parachute jumps, night vision capabilities, and stealthy movement to gain the element of surprise and disrupt enemy forces.

Air support played a crucial role in Operation Anaconda, and this subchapter explores the strategies employed to maximize its effectiveness. The integration of close air support, helicopter assaults, and tactical airstrikes ensured that Special Forces teams had the necessary firepower and mobility to accomplish their objectives. The use of advanced aircraft, such as Apache helicopters and AC-130 gunships, provided unparalleled firepower and precision strikes against enemy positions.

Intelligence gathering techniques were paramount to the success of Operation Anaconda, and this subchapter delves into the methods employed. Special Forces units utilized a combination of human intelligence, signals intelligence, and imagery intelligence to gather critical information about enemy positions, capabilities, and intentions. This intelligence was then used to plan and execute operations with maximum effectiveness.

The role of local Afghan militias in supporting Operation Anaconda cannot be understated. This subchapter explores the collaboration between U.S. Special Forces and these local forces, highlighting their invaluable contribution in providing intelligence, conducting reconnaissance, and engaging enemy fighters. Their knowledge of the local terrain and culture proved vital in achieving mission success.

Another critical aspect of Operation Anaconda was medical evacuation and field hospital operations. This subchapter examines the challenges faced by medical personnel in providing lifesaving care amidst hostile conditions. The establishment of field hospitals and evacuation procedures ensured that wounded soldiers received prompt medical attention, ultimately saving lives on the battlefield.

Analysis of the command and control structure in Operation Anaconda sheds light on the coordination between various military units involved in the operation. This subchapter explores the decentralized decision-making process that allowed Special Forces teams to adapt quickly to changing circumstances and exploit opportunities on the ground.

The use of advanced weaponry and technology in Operation Anaconda significantly enhanced the capabilities of Special Forces teams. This subchapter delves into the utilization of drones, advanced surveillance systems, and precision-guided munitions to gain a tactical advantage over the enemy.

Psychological operations and information warfare were critical components of Operation Anaconda. This subchapter explores how Special Forces teams employed psychological tactics and disseminated information to undermine enemy morale and disrupt their command and control structures.

Despite the primary objective being a military operation, Operation Anaconda also involved humanitarian assistance efforts. This subchapter highlights the efforts made by Special Forces to provide aid and support to local Afghan communities affected by the conflict.

Finally, this subchapter concludes with a comprehensive analysis of the lessons learned and strategic implications of Operation Anaconda for future military operations in Afghanistan. By understanding the successes and challenges faced during this operation, historians can glean valuable insights that can shape future military strategies and operations.

In conclusion, "Covert Operations and Infiltration Techniques Used by Special Forces" provides historians with a comprehensive understanding of the secretive and strategic methods employed during Operation Anaconda. By delving into the tactics, strategies, and lessons learned from this operation, historians can gain valuable insights for future military operations in Afghanistan.

Collaboration between Special Forces and Local Afghan Militias

In the complex and challenging terrain of Eastern Afghanistan, the success of Operation Anaconda hinged upon the crucial collaboration between the highly skilled U.S. Special Forces and the local Afghan militias. This subchapter explores the intricacies and significance of this partnership, shedding light on the critical role played by these Afghan militias in supporting the operation.

The Special Forces recognized the immense value of local knowledge, expertise, and relationships in executing their mission effectively. By forging alliances with Afghan militias, they tapped into a wellspring of intelligence and gained access to remote areas that would have otherwise remained inaccessible. These local fighters possessed an intimate understanding of the terrain, the people, and the dynamics of the region, proving to be invaluable assets for the success of Operation Anaconda.

The collaboration between the Special Forces and the Afghan militias was not without its challenges. Cultural and language barriers, as well as differences in operating procedures, required careful coordination and effective communication. The Special Forces had to bridge the gap, working closely with Afghan counterparts to establish trust, mutual respect, and a shared understanding of objectives. This collaboration was built on a foundation of respect for Afghan traditions and customs, reinforcing the message that Operation Anaconda was a joint effort aimed at liberating their homeland from the grip of terrorism.

This partnership also extended to the realm of tactical operations. The Afghan militias provided crucial local intelligence, identifying enemy hideouts, supply routes, and safe havens. Their intimate knowledge of the terrain allowed for precise targeting and effective ambushes, creating a significant advantage for the U.S. forces. Moreover, the Afghan militias, with their familiarity with the local populace, were able to gather intelligence from the communities, using their networks to identify potential threats and collaborators.

The collaboration between the Special Forces and the Afghan militias was a testament to the importance of understanding the local dynamics in conducting successful military operations. By leveraging the strengths of both parties and embracing a collaborative approach, Operation Anaconda achieved its objectives with remarkable efficiency.

This subchapter delves into the intricacies of this partnership, shedding light on the challenges faced, the strategies employed, and the ultimate success achieved through the collaboration between the Special Forces and the local Afghan militias. By analyzing this unique alliance, historians can draw valuable insights regarding the importance of local engagement, the significance of cultural understanding, and the potential benefits of collaborating with indigenous forces in future military operations in Afghanistan.

Chapter 3: Air Support Strategies Used in Operation Anaconda

Importance of Air Support in Eastern Afghanistan

Air support played a pivotal role in the success of Operation Anaconda, the 2002 U.S. Military Operation in Eastern Afghanistan. This subchapter aims to shed light on the significance of air support in this operation, discussing its impact and effectiveness in achieving the mission objectives. Historians, as well as scholars interested in various niches of Operation Anaconda, will find this information invaluable in understanding the intricacies of the operation.

The use of air support strategies was crucial in Operation Anaconda, as it provided the U.S. forces with a significant advantage over the enemy. The rugged and mountainous terrain of Eastern Afghanistan posed numerous challenges for ground forces, making it difficult to navigate and engage the enemy effectively. However, air support, including close air support (CAS), airlift capabilities, and reconnaissance, helped overcome these obstacles.

One of the key air support strategies employed in Operation Anaconda was the utilization of air power for intelligence gathering. Unmanned aerial vehicles (UAVs), such as drones, played a vital role in providing real-time situational awareness to ground forces, enabling them to identify enemy positions, movements, and potential threats. This intelligence was crucial for planning and executing successful operations.

Furthermore, the use of air support allowed for rapid medical evacuation and field hospital operations. The challenging terrain and the intensity of the enemy's resistance often resulted in casualties among the U.S. forces. Air support facilitated the swift evacuation of wounded soldiers to field hospitals, ensuring they received timely and life-saving medical treatment.

The command and control structure in Operation Anaconda heavily relied on air support assets. Advanced communication systems, including satellite communications and airborne command centers, enabled effective coordination and synchronization of military operations. This seamless integration of air support with ground forces enhanced the overall command and control capabilities, leading to successful mission execution.

Moreover, the use of advanced weaponry and technology, such as precision-guided munitions and night vision capabilities, further augmented the effectiveness of air support in Operation Anaconda. This advanced weaponry allowed for surgical strikes on enemy positions while minimizing collateral damage.

In addition to its combat effectiveness, air support also played a role in psychological operations and information warfare. The presence of aircraft overhead created a psychological impact on the enemy, disrupting their morale and forcing them to constantly remain vigilant. Furthermore, air support facilitated the dissemination of vital information and propaganda to local Afghan militias, garnering their support and cooperation.

Lastly, air support played a critical role in delivering humanitarian assistance during Operation Anaconda. Airlift capabilities enabled the transportation of essential supplies, including food, water, and medical aid, to remote and inaccessible areas of Eastern Afghanistan, ensuring the well-being of both the local population and U.S. forces.

In conclusion, the importance of air support in Operation Anaconda cannot be overstated. Its impact on intelligence gathering, command and control, medical evacuation, advanced weaponry, psychological operations, and humanitarian assistance was instrumental in achieving mission success. The lessons learned from Operation Anaconda will undoubtedly have strategic implications for future military operations in Afghanistan, making it imperative for historians and scholars to study and analyze this aspect of the operation.

Types of Aircraft and Missions Carried out during Operation Anaconda

Operation Anaconda was a significant military operation that took place in Eastern Afghanistan in 2002. It involved a complex and coordinated effort from various branches of the U.S. military, including special forces, air support, and intelligence gathering. A crucial aspect of the operation was the use of different types of aircraft to carry out specific missions.

One of the primary aircraft used during Operation Anaconda was the AH-64 Apache attack helicopter. These helicopters played a crucial role in providing close air support to ground forces. Equipped with advanced sensors and weapons systems, Apaches were able to engage enemy positions and provide valuable reconnaissance information to the command center. They were particularly effective in engaging enemy forces in rugged and mountainous terrain.

Another important aircraft utilized during the operation was the AC-130 gunship. This heavily armed ground-attack aircraft provided continuous and accurate fire support to the troops on the ground. The AC-130's sophisticated sensors and weapons, including cannons and Gatling guns, allowed it to engage targets with precision and accuracy, neutralizing enemy positions and providing cover for ground forces.

In addition to attack helicopters and gunships, transport aircraft such as the C-130 Hercules played a critical role in Operation Anaconda. These aircraft were responsible for deploying troops, equipment, and supplies to the battlefield. They also facilitated the medical evacuation of wounded soldiers, transporting them to field hospitals for immediate medical attention.

Furthermore, unmanned aerial vehicles (UAVs) played a crucial role in intelligence gathering during Operation Anaconda. These drones, equipped with high-resolution cameras and other surveillance equipment, provided real-time situational awareness to commanders. By conducting reconnaissance missions and collecting valuable intelligence, UAVs assisted in identifying enemy positions, tracking movements, and assessing the overall battlefield situation.

The diverse range of aircraft used during Operation Anaconda showcased the integration of air power with ground operations. These aircraft not only provided crucial air support but also contributed to intelligence gathering, troop deployment, and medical evacuation. The successful use of advanced weaponry and technology, combined with the coordination of different aircraft, played a pivotal role in the overall success of the operation.

The lessons learned from Operation Anaconda have strategic implications for future military operations in Afghanistan. The effective utilization of air support, intelligence gathering techniques, and the integration of advanced technology highlight the importance of a multi-dimensional approach in modern warfare. By understanding and analyzing the various aircraft used during Operation Anaconda, historians can gain valuable insights into the role of air power and its impact on military operations in Afghanistan.

Close Air Support and Bombing Campaigns in Support of Ground Forces

During Operation Anaconda, the U.S. military employed close air support and bombing campaigns to provide critical assistance to ground forces operating in Eastern Afghanistan. These strategies played a pivotal role in the success of the operation and had far-reaching implications for future military operations in the region.

In support of ground forces, close air support played a crucial role in eliminating enemy threats and providing cover for advancing troops. Special forces operating during Operation Anaconda relied heavily on close air support to neutralize enemy positions, disrupt enemy movements, and protect friendly forces. This close coordination between ground forces and air assets was essential in maintaining a tactical advantage and minimizing casualties.

In addition to close air support, bombing campaigns were carried out to target known enemy strongholds and disrupt their lines of communication. These campaigns involved precision strikes on enemy positions, infrastructure, and supply lines. By disrupting the enemy's ability to coordinate and resupply, these bombing campaigns significantly weakened their capabilities and bolstered the chances of success for ground forces.

To effectively carry out these air support strategies, extensive intelligence gathering techniques were employed. Gathering actionable intelligence was crucial in identifying enemy positions, determining their strength, and understanding their tactics. This intelligence was then used to plan and execute precise air strikes, minimizing collateral damage and maximizing the impact on enemy forces.

Local Afghan militias played a crucial role in supporting Operation Anaconda, particularly in providing intelligence and acting as liaisons between U.S. forces and the local population. Their knowledge of the terrain and understanding of local dynamics proved invaluable in the success of the operation.

Medical evacuation and field hospital operations were also an integral part of Operation Anaconda. The challenging terrain and hostile environment necessitated swift and efficient medical support. A comprehensive system was established to ensure the timely evacuation and treatment of wounded personnel, saving countless lives during the operation.

The command and control structure in Operation Anaconda was highly complex, involving multiple military branches and coalition forces. The coordination of air support and ground operations required meticulous planning and effective communication channels. Lessons learned from this operation have since been implemented to improve command and control structures in future military operations.

Advanced weaponry and technology played a significant role in Operation Anaconda. From precision-guided munitions to unmanned aerial vehicles, these advancements provided U.S. forces with a distinct advantage. The effective utilization of advanced technology allowed for enhanced reconnaissance, intelligence gathering, and precision strikes, ultimately contributing to the success of the operation.

Psychological operations and information warfare were also employed during Operation Anaconda. These tactics aimed to weaken enemy morale, disrupt their communication networks, and sway local populations in favor of U.S. forces. By leveraging information dissemination and psychological strategies, the U.S. military sought to gain a strategic advantage over the enemy.

Operation Anaconda also showcased the humanitarian assistance efforts of the U.S. military. Alongside combat operations, efforts were made to provide aid and support to the local population. This not only helped to win hearts and minds but also contributed to stability and security in the region.

In conclusion, the close air support and bombing campaigns employed during Operation Anaconda played a critical role in supporting ground forces and achieving success in Eastern Afghanistan. The lessons learned from this operation have had far-reaching strategic implications for future military operations in the region, informing the development of advanced tactics, technologies, and command structures. Operation Anaconda stands as a significant milestone in the ongoing efforts to ensure security and stability in Afghanistan.

Challenges and Limitations of Air Support in the Mountainous Terrain

In the rugged and treacherous terrain of the Eastern Afghanistan mountains, air support played a crucial role in the success of Operation Anaconda. However, this subchapter aims to shed light on the challenges and limitations faced by the U.S. military during this operation when it came to utilizing air support effectively.

One of the primary challenges encountered by the U.S. military was the unpredictable and harsh weather conditions prevalent in the mountainous terrain. The operation took place during the winter months when heavy snowfall and dense fog often hampered visibility and made it difficult for aircraft to navigate through the narrow valleys and steep slopes. These adverse weather conditions restricted the availability and effectiveness of air support, limiting the operational capabilities of the forces on the ground.

Furthermore, the mountainous landscape posed significant challenges for helicopter operations. The high altitudes and thin air reduced the lift capacity of helicopters, limiting the amount of personnel, equipment, and supplies that could be transported. Additionally, the mountain peaks and deep valleys created limited landing zones, forcing helicopters to hover or conduct vertical landings, making them vulnerable to enemy fire.

The enemy's effective use of anti-aircraft weaponry and tactics also posed a considerable threat to air support operations. The rugged terrain provided ample cover for the enemy to conceal their anti-aircraft systems, making it challenging for aircraft to identify and neutralize these threats. The fear of surface-to-air missiles and small arms fire forced helicopters to fly at higher altitudes, reducing their accuracy and increasing the risk of collateral damage.

Moreover, the vastness of the mountainous region and the scarcity of reliable intelligence sources made it difficult to pinpoint enemy positions accurately. The lack of real-time intelligence hindered the efficient deployment of air support, resulting in delayed response times and missed opportunities to provide timely assistance to ground forces.

Despite these challenges and limitations, the U.S. military employed various strategies to overcome these obstacles. They adapted their air support tactics by using precision-guided munitions and standoff weaponry to engage enemy positions from a safe distance. Additionally, they collaborated closely with special forces units on the ground to gather intelligence and direct air support accurately.

By analyzing the challenges and limitations faced during Operation Anaconda, historians and military strategists can gain valuable insights into the intricacies of conducting military operations in mountainous terrain. These lessons can help shape future military operations in Afghanistan and equip forces with the knowledge and strategies necessary to overcome the unique challenges posed by such environments.

Chapter 4: Intelligence Gathering Techniques Employed during Operation Anaconda

Role and Significance of Intelligence in Operation Anaconda

Intelligence played a pivotal role in the success of Operation Anaconda, the 2002 U.S. military operation in Eastern Afghanistan. During this challenging and complex mission, intelligence gathering techniques were employed to gather critical information, assess the enemy's capabilities and intentions, and provide accurate situational awareness to the commanders on the ground.

One of the key intelligence strategies used in Operation Anaconda was the utilization of advanced technology and weaponry. Unmanned aerial vehicles (UAVs) and satellite imagery provided real-time surveillance and reconnaissance capabilities, enabling the special forces to identify enemy positions, movements, and potential ambush sites. These technological advancements significantly enhanced the effectiveness and efficiency of the operation, reducing the risks faced by the U.S. military personnel.

Additionally, the intelligence community employed psychological operations and information warfare tactics to disrupt and degrade the enemy's morale and communication networks. By disseminating targeted propaganda and misinformation, the U.S. forces were able to sow confusion among the enemy ranks, making it harder for them to coordinate and mount effective counterattacks.

The role of local Afghan militias in supporting Operation Anaconda cannot be overstated. These Afghan forces, who had valuable knowledge of the region and its inhabitants, worked closely with intelligence operatives to gather information about enemy movements and provide insight into the local dynamics. Their involvement in intelligence gathering proved essential in identifying enemy hideouts, routes, and supply lines.

The command and control structure in Operation Anaconda was carefully analyzed to ensure efficient coordination and execution of the mission. Intelligence reports were shared among the various components of the operation, including special forces, air support, and field hospitals. This seamless flow of information facilitated timely decision-making and enabled the commanders to adapt their strategies based on the evolving threat landscape.

Furthermore, intelligence efforts were instrumental in supporting humanitarian assistance initiatives during Operation Anaconda. By understanding the local population's needs and vulnerabilities, aid organizations were able to provide targeted and effective support, mitigating the impact of the military operation on innocent civilians.

The lessons learned from Operation Anaconda have significant strategic implications for future military operations in Afghanistan. The importance of robust intelligence gathering and analysis cannot be overstated. It is crucial to invest in advanced technology, equip military personnel with the necessary training, and foster strong relationships with local partners to ensure the success of future operations.

In conclusion, intelligence played a vital and multifaceted role in Operation Anaconda. From gathering critical information to supporting command and control structures, intelligence efforts were instrumental in the success of the operation. The lessons learned from this operation will undoubtedly shape future military strategies in Afghanistan, ensuring more efficient and effective outcomes.

Human Intelligence (HUMINT) Operations in Eastern Afghanistan

During Operation Anaconda, the 2002 U.S. military operation in Eastern Afghanistan, Human Intelligence (HUMINT) operations played a critical role in gathering valuable information and intelligence on the enemy's activities, intentions, and capabilities. This subchapter aims to provide detailed insights into the HUMINT operations conducted during this operation, shedding light on the challenges faced, strategies employed, and the implications for future military operations in Afghanistan.

HUMINT operations in Eastern Afghanistan primarily involved covert activities carried out by highly trained Special Forces personnel. These operators infiltrated enemy territories, established relationships with local populations, and collected vital intelligence on insurgent hideouts, training camps, and supply routes. Their role was crucial in identifying high-value targets and disrupting the enemy's command and control structure.

The intelligence gathering techniques employed during Operation Anaconda were diverse and dynamic. Special Forces operators utilized a range of methods, including direct contact with local Afghan militias, engaging with key individuals within the enemy forces, and conducting covert surveillance and reconnaissance missions. These techniques enabled them to collect actionable intelligence and gain a deeper understanding of the enemy's tactics, strengths, and weaknesses.

The role of local Afghan militias cannot be underestimated in supporting HUMINT operations during Operation Anaconda. These militias, often referred to as "friendly forces," provided critical assistance to the U.S. military by acting as local informants, guides, and interpreters. Their deep knowledge of the terrain and familiarity with the local population proved invaluable in gathering intelligence and conducting successful operations against the enemy.

In terms of command and control structure, HUMINT operations were closely coordinated with other elements of the operation. Special Forces units worked hand in hand with air support assets, intelligence analysts, and field hospitals to ensure a seamless flow of information and efficient execution of missions. The advanced weaponry and technology used during Operation Anaconda further enhanced the effectiveness of HUMINT operations, enabling operators to transmit real-time intelligence and maintain constant situational awareness.

Furthermore, psychological operations and information warfare played a significant role in shaping the operational environment during Operation Anaconda. By leveraging media and propaganda, the U.S. military aimed to influence the perceptions and behaviors of both the enemy and the local population, gaining a psychological advantage in the conflict.

Lastly, Operation Anaconda also witnessed extensive humanitarian assistance efforts. The U.S. military, in coordination with international partners and non-governmental organizations, provided medical aid, food, water, and shelter to the civilian population affected by the conflict. These efforts not only helped alleviate the suffering of the local population but also served to win hearts and minds, ultimately contributing to the success of the operation.

In conclusion, HUMINT operations were vital components of Operation Anaconda, providing crucial intelligence and contributing to the achievement of operational objectives. The lessons learned from these operations, along with the strategic implications for future military operations in Afghanistan, will undoubtedly shape the future of warfare in this region. Understanding the challenges and successes of HUMINT operations in Eastern Afghanistan is essential for historians, as well as those interested in Special Forces operations, intelligence gathering techniques, and the overall dynamics of Operation Anaconda.

Signals Intelligence (SIGINT) and Electronic Warfare in Operation Anaconda

In the complex and intense battle of Operation Anaconda, Signals Intelligence (SIGINT) and Electronic Warfare played crucial roles in gathering vital information and disrupting enemy communications. This subchapter aims to shed light on the significance of SIGINT and Electronic Warfare during the 2002 U.S. Military Operation in Eastern Afghanistan.

Throughout Operation Anaconda, SIGINT operators employed sophisticated technology to intercept, analyze, and exploit enemy communications. By intercepting radio transmissions, cellular phone conversations, and other electronic signals, SIGINT teams obtained valuable intelligence on enemy movements, intentions, and capabilities. This information allowed U.S. forces to gain a tactical advantage by anticipating the enemy's next moves and adjusting their own strategies accordingly. In addition, SIGINT helped identify high-value targets, enabling the special forces to effectively neutralize key enemy leaders.

Electronic Warfare, on the other hand, focused on disrupting and degrading the enemy's communication systems and electronic devices. Electronic Warfare specialists employed various tactics such as jamming enemy radio signals, intercepting and manipulating enemy drones, and exploiting vulnerabilities in their electronic infrastructure. By disrupting enemy communications, Electronic Warfare significantly hindered their ability to coordinate attacks, gather intelligence, and maintain situational awareness. This disruption not only weakened the enemy's command and control structure but also created confusion and disarray among their ranks, ultimately contributing to the success of Operation Anaconda.

The integration of SIGINT and Electronic Warfare with other intelligence gathering techniques proved instrumental in the overall success of Operation Anaconda. By combining intercepted enemy communications with information obtained from human intelligence sources and aerial reconnaissance, a comprehensive and detailed picture of the battlefield was established. This fusion of intelligence allowed for effective target acquisition and ensured accurate and timely decision-making by commanders.

Furthermore, the use of advanced technology and weaponry in SIGINT and Electronic Warfare enhanced the capabilities of U.S. forces during Operation Anaconda. Cutting-edge surveillance equipment, drone technology, and cyber capabilities provided a significant edge in gathering intelligence and disrupting the enemy's communications. The ability to rapidly process and analyze large volumes of data allowed for real-time decision-making and increased operational effectiveness.

In conclusion, SIGINT and Electronic Warfare played critical roles in Operation Anaconda, providing the U.S. forces with a decisive advantage over the enemy. The integration of these capabilities with other intelligence gathering techniques, the use of advanced technology, and the disruption of enemy communications significantly contributed to the success of the operation. As historians analyze Operation Anaconda, it becomes evident that the effective utilization of SIGINT and Electronic Warfare serves as a valuable lesson for future military operations in Afghanistan.

Use of Unmanned Aerial Vehicles (UAVs) for Surveillance and Reconnaissance

Operation Anaconda: The Untold Story of the 2002 U.S. Military Operation in Eastern Afghanistan delves into the intricacies of this significant military campaign. As historians dissect the various aspects of Operation Anaconda, one crucial element that cannot be overlooked is the use of Unmanned Aerial Vehicles (UAVs) for surveillance and reconnaissance. These cutting-edge technologies revolutionized the way intelligence was gathered, providing invaluable support to the troops on the ground.

During Operation Anaconda, UAVs played a pivotal role in providing real-time situational awareness to the U.S. military forces. Equipped with high-resolution cameras, these unmanned aircraft operated at various altitudes, capturing vital imagery and video footage of the battlefield. This visual data proved instrumental in identifying enemy positions, monitoring their movements, and assessing the effectiveness of airstrikes.

The Special Forces operating during Operation Anaconda greatly benefited from the use of UAVs. These elite units, tasked with executing complex missions in hostile environments, relied on the real-time intelligence gathered by UAVs to plan their operations meticulously. The ability to survey the terrain from above gave them a significant advantage, enabling them to navigate rugged landscapes, avoid potential ambushes, and identify enemy strongholds.

Furthermore, the integration of UAVs with air support strategies amplified their effectiveness. The intelligence gathered by these unmanned aircraft directly influenced the decisions made by air assets, such as attack helicopters and fighter jets. The ability to accurately locate and engage enemy targets, while minimizing collateral damage, was greatly enhanced through the use of UAVs.

In addition to their role in surveillance and reconnaissance, UAVs also played a critical role in supporting medical evacuation and field hospital operations during Operation Anaconda. These unmanned aircraft provided a rapid and efficient means of transporting injured personnel from the battlefield to medical facilities, saving countless lives in the process.

The lessons learned from the use of UAVs in Operation Anaconda have profound strategic implications for future military operations in

Afghanistan. The success of these unmanned aircraft in providing real-time intelligence and enhancing operational capabilities highlights the need for continued investment in advanced technologies. As the U.S. military continues its presence in Afghanistan, the use of UAVs for surveillance and reconnaissance will remain a vital component of intelligence gathering, ensuring the safety and effectiveness of military operations.

In conclusion, the use of Unmanned Aerial Vehicles (UAVs) for surveillance and reconnaissance during Operation Anaconda proved to be a game-changer. The integration of these cutting-edge technologies provided real-time situational awareness, enhanced the effectiveness of air support strategies, and facilitated medical evacuation operations. As historians analyze the intricacies of Operation Anaconda, it is vital to recognize the pivotal role that UAVs played in shaping the outcome of this significant military campaign.

Chapter 5: Role of Local Afghan Militias in Supporting Operation Anaconda

Collaboration between U.S. Forces and Local Afghan Militias

One of the key elements that enabled the success of Operation Anaconda, the 2002 U.S. military operation in Eastern Afghanistan, was the collaboration between U.S. forces and local Afghan militias. This subchapter delves into the significance of this alliance, highlighting its impact on the outcome of the operation.

The U.S. military recognized the importance of working closely with local Afghan militias, as they possessed invaluable knowledge of the terrain, culture, and the enemy's tactics. These militias, composed of Afghan fighters who were familiar with the region, played a crucial role in gathering intelligence and providing essential support to the U.S. forces.

During Operation Anaconda, the collaboration between the U.S. forces and local Afghan militias proved to be a force multiplier. The Afghan militias acted as a bridge between the U.S. military and the local population, establishing trust and rapport with the Afghan communities. This connection enabled the U.S. forces to gain critical insights into the enemy's movements, hideouts, and supply lines.

The local Afghan militias proved to be highly effective in engaging the enemy forces. Their knowledge of the terrain allowed them to navigate through the rugged and treacherous Afghan mountains, providing the U.S. forces with invaluable guidance. Additionally, the militias' understanding of the local culture and language facilitated communication and cooperation between the U.S. forces and the Afghan population, ultimately aiding in the identification and neutralization of hostile elements.

The collaboration between the U.S. forces and local Afghan militias extended beyond combat operations. The militias played a vital role in facilitating humanitarian assistance efforts during Operation Anaconda. Their knowledge of the local communities enabled the U.S. forces to identify areas in need of aid and distribute essential supplies effectively.

This partnership between the U.S. forces and local Afghan militias had a profound impact on the command and control structure of Operation Anaconda. The integration of local militias into the U.S. military's decision-making process allowed for a more comprehensive and nuanced understanding of the operational environment. The input provided by the Afghan militias influenced tactical decisions, contributing to the overall success of the mission.

The collaboration between U.S. forces and local Afghan militias during Operation Anaconda showcased the power of combining local knowledge with advanced military capabilities. This alliance not only contributed to the operational success of the mission but also fostered trust and cooperation between the U.S. military and the Afghan population.

The lessons learned from this collaboration have significant strategic implications for future military operations in Afghanistan. The success of Operation Anaconda highlights the importance of building strong partnerships with local forces and leveraging their expertise to achieve operational objectives. This invaluable experience will undoubtedly shape the approach of future U.S. military operations in Afghanistan, emphasizing the significance of collaboration with local Afghan militias.

Recruitment, Training, and Integration of Afghan Militias

The successful execution of Operation Anaconda in Eastern Afghanistan in 2002 relied heavily on the recruitment, training, and integration of local Afghan militias. This subchapter delves into the crucial role played by these militias in supporting the mission's objectives and highlights their unique contributions to the overall success of the operation.

Recruitment of Afghan militias was a painstaking process that required careful vetting and selection. Special forces units, operating in close coordination with intelligence agencies, identified individuals with a deep understanding of the local terrain, culture, and insurgent networks. These individuals, often former mujahideen or members of anti-Taliban factions, proved invaluable in gathering intelligence, conducting reconnaissance, and engaging with the local population.

Once recruited, the training of Afghan militias was conducted through a comprehensive program designed to enhance their combat effectiveness. Special forces trainers, drawing upon their expertise in unconventional warfare, imparted crucial skills such as small unit tactics, marksmanship, and combat first aid. This training not only improved the militias' ability to engage the enemy but also instilled a sense of confidence and professionalism within their ranks.

Integration of the Afghan militias into the broader operational structure of Operation Anaconda was a key challenge. To foster effective coordination and cooperation, liaison officers were embedded within the militias, facilitating the flow of information and ensuring alignment with the overall mission objectives. Regular joint exercises and training sessions were conducted to enhance interoperability between U.S. and Afghan forces, instilling a sense of camaraderie and shared purpose.

The role of local Afghan militias in supporting Operation Anaconda cannot be overstated. These militias provided critical intelligence on enemy positions, supply lines, and safe havens, thereby enabling precision strikes and disrupting insurgent operations. Their intimate knowledge of the local population also facilitated the establishment of trust and cooperation, leading to valuable information and the identification of potential sympathizers.

Furthermore, the Afghan militias played a crucial role in securing and stabilizing areas liberated from insurgent control. Their presence and engagement with the local population helped establish a sense of security and deterrence against insurgent reprisals. This allowed for the initiation of humanitarian assistance efforts, providing much-needed support to the local population and demonstrating the positive impact of Operation Anaconda.

In conclusion, the recruitment, training, and integration of Afghan militias were pivotal components of Operation Anaconda's success. The unique capabilities and local knowledge they brought to the table greatly enhanced the operational effectiveness of U.S. and allied forces. The lessons learned from this experience have significant strategic implications for future military operations in Afghanistan, emphasizing the importance of leveraging and empowering local partners in counterinsurgency campaigns.

Contributions and Challenges Faced by Afghan Militias in Eastern Afghanistan

Introduction:

The subchapter "Contributions and Challenges Faced by Afghan Militias in Eastern Afghanistan" explores the crucial role played by local Afghan militias during Operation Anaconda in 2002. This section delves into the contributions made by these militias, as well as the challenges they encountered, shedding light on the complex dynamics of the operation. By examining the experiences of these Afghan fighters, historians can gain valuable insights into the effectiveness of militia support and the difficulties faced in utilizing their capabilities.

Contributions of Afghan Militias:

The contributions of Afghan militias were instrumental in the success of Operation Anaconda. These local fighters possessed an intimate knowledge of the rugged terrain, intricate network of caves, and hidden enemy positions. Their familiarity with the local culture, languages, and customs enabled them to gather vital intelligence, providing a significant advantage to the U.S. military forces.

Furthermore, the Afghan militias played a crucial role in facilitating communication and cooperation between U.S. Special Forces and the local population. Their ability to build trust and relationships with Afghan communities proved invaluable in gaining local support and assistance, which was vital for gathering intelligence and identifying enemy combatants.

Challenges Faced by Afghan Militias:

While the Afghan militias made substantial contributions, they also faced numerous challenges during Operation Anaconda. One key challenge was their limited access to advanced weaponry and technology, which put them at a disadvantage against well-equipped enemy forces. This issue highlighted the need for greater support and resources to enhance the effectiveness of the militias.

Another challenge encountered by Afghan militias was the constant threat of reprisals from enemy fighters. The militias often found themselves targeted by insurgent groups, jeopardizing their safety and hindering their ability to carry out their tasks effectively. This highlighted the importance of providing adequate protection and support for these local fighters.

Conclusion:

The contributions and challenges faced by Afghan militias in Eastern Afghanistan during Operation Anaconda were pivotal and deserve recognition. These local fighters played a vital role in gathering intelligence, building relationships with the local population, and supporting U.S. military forces. However, they also faced significant challenges, including limited access to advanced weaponry and the constant threat of reprisals. Understanding the experiences of Afghan militias provides historians with valuable insights into the dynamics of Operation Anaconda and emphasizes the need for continued support and resources to empower local forces in future military operations in Afghanistan.

Chapter 6: Medical Evacuation and Field Hospital Operations during Operation Anaconda

Importance of Medical Support in Combat Operations

In the midst of the chaos and violence that characterizes combat operations, the importance of medical support cannot be overstated. It is a critical aspect that ensures the well-being and survival of both military personnel and civilians caught in the crossfire. Operation Anaconda, the 2002 U.S. Military Operation in Eastern Afghanistan, witnessed the pivotal role played by medical support in saving lives and maintaining morale.

During Operation Anaconda, special forces operated under extreme conditions, often in remote and hostile terrains. The success of these operations relied heavily on the availability of medical support. Special forces operators frequently engaged in close-quarter combat, risking severe injuries that required immediate medical attention. The presence of highly skilled medics and medical personnel ensured that wounded soldiers received prompt treatment and were stabilized for evacuation.

Air support strategies were deployed throughout Operation Anaconda to provide cover and facilitate medical evacuation. Helicopters, equipped with medical facilities, were utilized to airlift wounded soldiers to field hospitals where they could receive advanced medical care. These air support strategies were instrumental in reducing the time between injury and treatment, significantly increasing the chances of survival.

Effective intelligence gathering techniques were paramount in identifying and neutralizing enemy threats. Medical support played a crucial role in this process by providing detailed medical assessments of captured enemy combatants. These assessments helped intelligence teams understand the enemy's capabilities, weaknesses, and potential strategies, enabling more effective planning and execution of future operations.

Local Afghan militias played a vital role in supporting Operation Anaconda. However, their limited medical capabilities meant that the burden of providing medical support fell on the U.S. military. Field hospitals were established near the frontlines, equipped with state-of-the-art medical equipment and staffed by highly trained medical professionals. These field hospitals acted as a lifeline, providing immediate care to injured soldiers before being transported to more advanced medical facilities.

The command and control structure during Operation Anaconda heavily relied on the seamless coordination of medical support. Medical personnel were integrated into the command structure, ensuring that decisions were made with the well-being of soldiers in mind. This integration facilitated the efficient allocation of medical resources and allowed for flexible responses to evolving situations.

Modern warfare heavily relies on advanced weaponry and technology, and Operation Anaconda was no exception. Medical support adapted to these advancements by employing advanced medical techniques and equipment. From advanced imaging systems for rapid diagnosis to telemedicine capabilities for remote consultations, medical support ensured that soldiers received the best possible care.

In a psychological warfare-infused environment, medical support played a crucial role in maintaining morale among troops. Timely and effective medical care not only saved lives but also provided a sense of security and confidence to soldiers operating in challenging circumstances. Knowing that medical support was readily available boosted the morale of troops and allowed them to focus on the mission at hand.

Operation Anaconda was not just about combat operations; it also involved humanitarian assistance efforts. Medical support played a vital role in these efforts by providing medical care to displaced civilians and building trust between the local population and the U.S. military. These efforts were instrumental in winning the hearts and minds of the Afghan people.

The lessons learned from Operation Anaconda have significant strategic implications for future military operations in Afghanistan. The importance of robust medical support cannot be overlooked. Adequate resources, training, and coordination are essential to ensure the success of combat operations and the overall mission.

In conclusion, medical support is a critical component of combat operations. It saves lives, maintains morale, and facilitates the success of mission objectives. Operation Anaconda highlighted the pivotal role played by medical support in the face of adversity. The lessons learned from this operation must be heeded for future military operations in Afghanistan and beyond.

Establishment and Organization of Field Hospitals in Eastern Afghanistan

During Operation Anaconda in 2002, the establishment and organization of field hospitals played a critical role in providing medical support to the U.S. military forces and local Afghan populations in Eastern Afghanistan. This subchapter aims to shed light on the significant efforts made in this aspect of the operation, addressing the interests of historians and various niches related to Operation Anaconda.

Field hospitals were strategically positioned in close proximity to the combat zones to ensure swift medical intervention and enhance the chances of survival for injured personnel. These hospitals were staffed with highly trained medical professionals, including doctors, nurses, and medics, who worked tirelessly to save lives in the midst of a challenging operational environment. The subchapter will explore the challenges faced by medical teams, such as limited resources, harsh weather conditions, and the constant threat of enemy attacks.

The content will also delve into the organization and logistics of field hospitals, highlighting their ability to provide comprehensive medical care. This will include discussions on the triage system used to prioritize patients based on the severity of their injuries, the availability of surgical facilities for emergency procedures, and the efficient evacuation of casualties to higher-level medical facilities when necessary.

Furthermore, the subchapter will examine the collaboration between U.S. military medical personnel and local Afghan militias in providing medical assistance to the local population. This cooperation was instrumental in building trust and fostering positive relations between the U.S. forces and the Afghan communities. The content will delve into the specific roles played by local Afghan militias in supporting field hospitals, such as providing security, acting as interpreters, and assisting in the identification and treatment of patients.

The subchapter will also touch upon the lessons learned from the establishment and organization of field hospitals during Operation Anaconda. It will discuss the strategic implications of these lessons for future military operations in Afghanistan, addressing the concerns of historians and those interested in the future of warfare.

In conclusion, the establishment and organization of field hospitals in Eastern Afghanistan during Operation Anaconda played a pivotal role in providing critical medical support to both U.S. military forces and local Afghan populations. This subchapter will explore the challenges faced, the organizational strategies implemented, and the lessons learned from this aspect of the operation, catering to the interests of historians and the various niches related to Operation Anaconda.

Challenges and Successes of Medical Evacuation Operations

In the midst of the intense and complex military operation that was Operation Anaconda in Eastern Afghanistan in 2002, medical evacuation operations played a vital role in ensuring the survival and recovery of injured personnel. These operations faced numerous challenges, but ultimately achieved remarkable success in saving lives and providing critical care to those in need.

One of the major challenges faced by medical evacuation teams during Operation Anaconda was the hostile and rugged terrain of the Afghan mountains. The difficult terrain made it extremely challenging to reach and extract wounded soldiers quickly and safely. The remote locations and harsh weather conditions added further complications to the evacuation process. Despite these obstacles, the medical evacuation teams displayed exceptional skill and determination, overcoming the odds to bring injured personnel to safety.

Another significant challenge was the threat of enemy fire. The Taliban fighters, aware of the importance of medical evacuation operations, targeted these vulnerable aircraft and personnel. This necessitated the implementation of robust security measures to protect the helicopters and medical staff during evacuation missions. The success of these operations relied heavily on the close coordination between the medical teams and the special forces providing security cover.

Despite these challenges, the medical evacuation operations during Operation Anaconda achieved remarkable success. The coordination and integration of various military assets such as helicopters, fixed-wing aircraft, and field hospitals, ensured the smooth flow of injured personnel from the battlefield to advanced medical care. The use of advanced technologies and equipment, such as night vision goggles and state-of-the-art medical equipment, further enhanced the effectiveness of these operations.

The timely evacuation and medical treatment provided by these operations significantly increased the chances of survival for the wounded soldiers. The establishment of field hospitals near the frontlines allowed for immediate stabilization and surgical intervention, minimizing the risk of complications and long-term disabilities.

The successes of the medical evacuation operations during Operation Anaconda highlight the importance of a well-coordinated and integrated approach to battlefield medicine. The lessons learned from this operation have had strategic implications for future military operations in Afghanistan. The need for specialized training for medical personnel in combat situations, the development of innovative evacuation techniques, and the continued investment in advanced medical technologies have all been recognized as critical factors in ensuring the success of future operations.

In conclusion, the challenges faced by medical evacuation operations during Operation Anaconda were significant, but the successes achieved were equally remarkable. The dedication, skill, and bravery of the medical personnel involved played a crucial role in saving lives and providing critical care in one of the most challenging environments imaginable. The lessons learned from this operation will undoubtedly shape the future of military medical operations in Afghanistan and beyond.

Chapter 7: Analysis of the Command and Control Structure in Operation Anaconda

Overview of the Command Structure in Operation Anaconda

In the book "Operation Anaconda: The Untold Story of the 2002 U.S. Military Operation in Eastern Afghanistan," it is crucial for historians and those interested in Operation Anaconda to understand the command structure that played a vital role in the mission's success. The command structure ensured coordination, communication, and effective decision-making throughout the operation.

Operation Anaconda, a significant military operation conducted in Eastern Afghanistan in 2002, involved various units and forces working together under a centralized command structure. The operation aimed to disrupt and defeat insurgent groups in the region, primarily targeting Al-Qaeda and Taliban forces.

At the helm of the command structure was General John T. Nicholson, the overall commander of the operation. He was responsible for the strategic planning, resource allocation, and coordination of all forces involved. General Nicholson's expertise and experience in counterinsurgency operations proved instrumental in achieving the mission's objectives.

Under General Nicholson's command, several specialized units played crucial roles in Operation Anaconda. Special forces, including U.S. Army Green Berets and Navy SEALs, conducted covert operations, intelligence gathering, and direct action against high-value targets. Their expertise in unconventional warfare and close-quarters combat proved invaluable in the complex terrain of Eastern Afghanistan.

Air support played a vital role in Operation Anaconda, and the command structure ensured effective integration of air assets into the overall mission plan. The use of advanced air support strategies, such as close air support and precision airstrikes, provided cover, firepower, and reconnaissance capabilities to ground forces. This coordination significantly enhanced the effectiveness and success of the operation.

Intelligence gathering techniques played a critical role in Operation Anaconda. The command structure facilitated the collection, analysis, and dissemination of actionable intelligence. This intelligence, obtained through various means such as signals intelligence, human intelligence, and aerial reconnaissance, enabled commanders to make informed decisions and effectively target enemy forces.

Local Afghan militias played a significant role in supporting Operation Anaconda. The command structure facilitated coordination and cooperation with these militias, leveraging their knowledge of the local terrain, culture, and enemy networks. Their assistance proved crucial in identifying insurgent strongholds, gathering intelligence, and conducting joint operations.

Medical evacuation and field hospital operations were paramount during Operation Anaconda. The command structure ensured the rapid and efficient evacuation of wounded personnel to advanced medical facilities. This timely medical support saved numerous lives and boosted the morale of the forces involved.

The command and control structure in Operation Anaconda was characterized by effective communication, decentralized decision-making, and efficient coordination among different units and forces. This structure allowed for flexibility in adapting to changing circumstances and enabled the exploitation of emerging opportunities on the battlefield.

The use of advanced weaponry and technology played a pivotal role in Operation Anaconda. The command structure facilitated the integration and deployment of cutting-edge equipment, including unmanned aerial vehicles, precision-guided munitions, and advanced communication systems. These technological advancements significantly enhanced the operational capabilities of the forces involved.

Psychological operations and information warfare were key components of Operation Anaconda. The command structure ensured the dissemination of accurate information to the local population, aimed at winning hearts and minds and countering enemy propaganda. These operations played a crucial role in maintaining stability, building trust, and undermining the insurgents' influence.

Humanitarian assistance efforts were also an integral part of Operation Anaconda. The command structure facilitated the delivery of aid, medical support, and infrastructure development projects to win the support of the local population and improve their quality of life. These efforts helped build trust, cooperation, and long-term stability in the region.

Analyzing the command structure, lessons learned, and strategic implications of Operation Anaconda provides valuable insights for future military operations in Afghanistan. Understanding the successes, challenges, and operational dynamics of this mission is crucial in developing effective strategies and tactics for future counterinsurgency operations.

In conclusion, the command structure in Operation Anaconda played a vital role in the success of the mission. It enabled effective coordination, communication, and decision-making among various units and forces involved. The integration of specialized units, advanced technology, and the support of local Afghan militias were key components of the command structure. This overview provides historians and those interested in Operation Anaconda with a comprehensive understanding of the command structure's significance in achieving the mission's objectives.

Integration and Coordination between Different Units and Agencies

In the book "Operation Anaconda: The Untold Story of the 2002 U.S. Military Operation in Eastern Afghanistan," one of the crucial aspects that emerges is the effective integration and coordination between different units and agencies involved in the operation. This chapter explores the intricate web of collaboration and synchronization that enabled the success of Operation Anaconda.

The 2002 U.S. Military Operation in Eastern Afghanistan was a complex and multifaceted endeavor that required seamless coordination between various military units, intelligence agencies, and local Afghan militias. This integration was crucial for the success of the operation, as it ensured effective communication, resource allocation, and strategic decision-making.

At the heart of this integration were the Special Forces operations during Operation Anaconda. These highly skilled and adaptable units played a significant role in bridging the gap between different agencies and units. Their expertise in unconventional warfare tactics and their ability to work closely with local Afghan militias proved invaluable in achieving the mission objectives.

Furthermore, the successful execution of Operation Anaconda relied heavily on robust air support strategies. The coordination between ground units and air assets, such as helicopters and drones, was crucial in providing timely and accurate reconnaissance, close air support, and troop transport. The integration of air power into the overall operational plan ensured that ground forces had the necessary support and firepower to overcome the challenges they faced.

Effective intelligence gathering techniques were also instrumental in the success of Operation Anaconda. The integration of intelligence agencies, such as the CIA and NSA, with military units allowed for the collection and analysis of critical information. This intelligence was used to identify enemy positions, assess their capabilities, and anticipate their movements, providing a significant advantage to the U.S. forces.

The role of local Afghan militias cannot be overlooked when discussing integration and coordination. These militias, with their knowledge of the local terrain and communities, provided crucial support to the U.S. forces. Their integration into the overall operational plan enabled effective collaboration and enhanced situational awareness.

Another aspect that played a vital role in the success of Operation Anaconda was the seamless coordination of medical evacuation and field hospital operations. The integration of medical units and assets ensured that injured personnel received prompt and effective medical care, minimizing casualties and bolstering the morale of the troops.

The analysis of the command and control structure in Operation Anaconda reveals the importance of effective coordination and communication between different units and agencies. The integration of command elements, such as the Joint Special Operations Command (JSOC) and the Central Command (CENTCOM), facilitated the dissemination of orders, the allocation of resources, and the synchronization of efforts.

The use of advanced weaponry and technology was another crucial aspect of integration. The integration of cutting-edge surveillance systems, precision-guided munitions, and networked communication systems enhanced the effectiveness and efficiency of the operation. This integration allowed for real-time information sharing and improved situational awareness.

Psychological operations and information warfare also played a significant role in Operation Anaconda. The integration of these elements into the overall operational plan allowed for the dissemination of crucial information, shaping the perception of the enemy and influencing local populations. This integration was essential in gaining the support of local communities and delegitimizing the enemy's narrative.

Operation Anaconda was not only a military operation but also involved humanitarian assistance efforts. The integration of humanitarian organizations and resources allowed for the provision of essential services to the local Afghan population, enhancing the overall success of the mission and contributing to the hearts-and-minds campaign.

Finally, the lessons learned and strategic implications of Operation Anaconda for future military operations in Afghanistan cannot be understated. The successful integration and coordination between different units and agencies during Operation Anaconda provide valuable insights into how future operations can be planned and executed.

In conclusion, the integration and coordination between different units and agencies played a pivotal role in the success of Operation Anaconda. The seamless collaboration between Special Forces, air support assets, intelligence agencies, local Afghan militias, and humanitarian organizations ensured effective communication, resource allocation, and strategic decision-making. The lessons learned from this operation have far-reaching implications for future military operations in Afghanistan and provide valuable insights for historians and niche audiences interested in Operation Anaconda and related topics.

Decision-Making Processes and Communication Systems

In the high-stakes environment of military operations, effective decision-making processes and communication systems play a pivotal role in determining the success or failure of a mission. Operation Anaconda, the 2002 U.S. military operation in Eastern Afghanistan, exemplified the critical importance of these elements in achieving mission objectives while minimizing risks and casualties. This subchapter delves into the intricate web of decision-making processes and communication systems that were employed during Operation Anaconda, providing valuable insights for historians and specialists in various niches related to this operation.

From the outset, Operation Anaconda faced numerous challenges, including a formidable enemy, difficult terrain, and complex operational requirements. To navigate these challenges, the U.S. military relied on a well-defined decision-making process, characterized by a hierarchical structure that integrated inputs from various sources. This process involved the careful analysis of intelligence reports, which were gathered through sophisticated techniques such as signal intelligence and human intelligence. The inputs from specialized units, such as special forces, were also crucial in shaping the decision-making process.

Effective communication systems were the lifelines of Operation Anaconda. The operation required seamless coordination among multiple units, including ground forces, air support, and intelligence gathering teams. To achieve this, various communication technologies were employed, ranging from advanced radios to satellite systems. These systems enabled real-time sharing of critical information, enhancing situational awareness and providing commanders with the necessary insights to make informed decisions.

Furthermore, the command and control structure in Operation Anaconda was designed to optimize decision-making and communication processes. The establishment of a centralized command center facilitated the coordination of different units and ensured a unified approach to the mission. This structure allowed for rapid dissemination of orders, real-time updates, and efficient allocation of resources.

The use of advanced weaponry and technology also had a significant impact on decision-making processes and communication systems. Precision-guided munitions, unmanned aerial vehicles, and other cutting-edge tools enabled the U.S. military to gather intelligence, engage enemy forces, and provide air support with unprecedented accuracy. The integration of these advanced capabilities into the decision-making process and communication systems amplified the effectiveness of Operation Anaconda.

In conclusion, Operation Anaconda showcased the vital role of decision-making processes and communication systems in military operations. The careful analysis of intelligence, effective coordination among units, and the use of advanced technology were crucial factors in the success of this operation. Historians and specialists in various niches related to Operation Anaconda can draw valuable lessons from the decision-making processes and communication systems employed, refining their understanding of this operation and its strategic implications for future military operations in Afghanistan.

Chapter 8: Use of Advanced Weaponry and Technology in Operation Anaconda

Introduction to Advanced Weaponry and Technology Deployed in Eastern Afghanistan

In the highly complex and volatile theater of Eastern Afghanistan during Operation Anaconda in 2002, the United States military deployed an array of advanced weaponry and technology to gain a decisive advantage against the Taliban and other insurgent groups. This subchapter provides an overview of the cutting-edge tools and tactics employed during the operation, shedding light on the significant role they played in achieving the mission's objectives.

The deployment of advanced weaponry and technology was a crucial aspect of Operation Anaconda, enabling the U.S. military to counter the adversaries' asymmetric warfare tactics effectively. This included the use of unmanned aerial vehicles (UAVs), such as armed drones, which provided real-time intelligence, surveillance, and reconnaissance capabilities. These UAVs offered an unprecedented advantage by collecting critical information and targeting enemy combatants accurately, minimizing risks to U.S. forces.

Additionally, the U.S. military utilized cutting-edge infantry weapons, including advanced assault rifles with enhanced accuracy and firepower. These weapons allowed the American forces to engage the enemy effectively and maintain a tactical advantage in intense firefights. Furthermore, the deployment of precision-guided munitions, such as laser-guided bombs and missiles, significantly reduced collateral damage and civilian casualties while maximizing the destruction of enemy targets.

The operation also witnessed the deployment of advanced communication and command systems, enabling seamless coordination between various units and facilitating rapid decision-making. This sophisticated command and control structure ensured effective integration of ground forces, special operations units, and air support assets, leading to a cohesive and synchronized effort against the insurgents.

Moreover, psychological operations and information warfare played a crucial role in shaping the narrative surrounding Operation Anaconda. Advanced technology allowed the U.S. military to conduct targeted information campaigns, disseminating accurate and timely information to counter enemy propaganda and win the hearts and minds of the local population.

As historians, it is essential to recognize the pivotal role played by advanced weaponry and technology in Operation Anaconda. The successful integration of these assets into the military strategy enhanced the effectiveness, efficiency, and survivability of U.S. forces. Lessons learned from this operation can provide valuable insights for future military operations in Afghanistan and beyond, emphasizing the significance of staying at the forefront of technological advancements to ensure mission success and minimize risks to military personnel and civilians alike.

In conclusion, the deployment of advanced weaponry and technology in Eastern Afghanistan during Operation Anaconda revolutionized the way the U.S. military conducted combat operations. From UAVs and precision-guided munitions to advanced communication systems, these tools proved instrumental in achieving the mission's objectives. Understanding the utilization and impact of this advanced technology provides historians with valuable insights into the evolution of modern warfare and the strategic implications for future military operations in Afghanistan and beyond.

Role and Impact of Drones and Surveillance Systems

As historians delve into the intricate details of Operation Anaconda, it becomes evident that the role and impact of drones and surveillance systems played a pivotal part in the success of this military operation. The integration of advanced technology, such as unmanned aerial vehicles (UAVs) and cutting-edge surveillance systems, revolutionized the way intelligence was gathered, targets were identified, and situational awareness was maintained.

During Operation Anaconda, the deployment of drones provided a bird's-eye view of the battlefield, enabling commanders to analyze the terrain, identify enemy positions, and assess potential threats. These unmanned aircraft acted as the eyes in the sky, providing real-time video feeds and high-resolution imagery, which were then relayed to ground troops and command centers. The ability to gather actionable intelligence from the air significantly enhanced the effectiveness and efficiency of the U.S. military's operations.

Moreover, the utilization of surveillance systems, both on the ground and in the air, allowed for constant monitoring of the enemy's movements, communications, and activities. This comprehensive surveillance network played a crucial role in tracking and neutralizing high-value targets, disrupting enemy supply lines, and preempting potential ambushes. By leveraging advanced technology, the U.S. military was able to gain a significant tactical advantage, mitigating risks and minimizing casualties.

The impact of drones and surveillance systems extended beyond the immediate battlefield. These technological advancements facilitated a deeper understanding of the local Afghan militias and their role in supporting Operation Anaconda. By monitoring their interactions, movements, and affiliations, the U.S. military was able to foster stronger alliances and leverage the local knowledge and expertise of these Afghan militias. This collaboration proved invaluable in gathering intelligence, identifying safe havens for enemy combatants, and disrupting their operations.

In addition, the integration of drones and surveillance systems played a crucial role in the humanitarian assistance efforts during Operation Anaconda. The ability to assess the needs of affected communities, identify areas requiring urgent medical attention, and coordinate the delivery of aid was greatly enhanced by the use of technology. By leveraging these advanced tools, the U.S. military was able to provide timely and targeted humanitarian assistance, alleviating suffering and fostering goodwill among the local population.

Looking ahead, the lessons learned from the role and impact of drones and surveillance systems in Operation Anaconda have significant strategic implications for future military operations in Afghanistan. The successful integration of advanced technology underscores the importance of investing in research and development, training, and infrastructure to maintain a technological edge. Furthermore, it highlights the need for a holistic approach to intelligence gathering, combining human intelligence, signals intelligence, and technological capabilities to build a comprehensive and accurate picture of the battlefield.

In conclusion, the role and impact of drones and surveillance systems were instrumental in the success of Operation Anaconda. By providing real-time intelligence, enhancing situational awareness, and enabling targeted strikes, these technologies revolutionized the way the U.S. military operated in Eastern Afghanistan. The lessons learned from their implementation will undoubtedly shape future military operations, ensuring the U.S. maintains a competitive advantage in the ever-evolving landscape of modern warfare.

Precision-guided Munitions and Targeting Systems

In the midst of the intense and complex military operation known as Operation Anaconda, precision-guided munitions and targeting systems played a pivotal role in achieving success on the battlefield. This subchapter delves into the criticality of these advanced technologies and their impact on the outcome of the 2002 U.S. Military Operation in Eastern Afghanistan. Aimed at historians and specialists interested in Operation Anaconda, this subchapter aims to shed light on the strategic implications and lessons learned from the utilization of precision-guided munitions and targeting systems.

Throughout Operation Anaconda, the U.S. Special Forces relied heavily on precision-guided munitions to accurately strike enemy positions while minimizing collateral damage. These weapons, equipped with advanced guidance systems, enabled the military to target specific objectives with pinpoint accuracy, even in difficult terrains and adverse weather conditions. The integration of these munitions into the operation significantly enhanced the effectiveness of U.S. air support strategies by reducing the risk to friendly forces and maximizing the destruction of enemy assets.

Furthermore, the success of Operation Anaconda was also heavily dependent on sophisticated targeting systems. These systems, leveraging cutting-edge technology, provided real-time intelligence on enemy movements and positions, enabling commanders to make informed decisions on the allocation of resources and the execution of military actions. By harnessing the power of these targeting systems, the U.S. military was able to minimize the element of surprise for the enemy and maintain a tactical advantage throughout the operation.

The utilization of precision-guided munitions and targeting systems was further complemented by the expertise and intelligence gathered during Operation Anaconda. The integration of local Afghan militias, with their knowledge of the terrain and the enemy, proved invaluable in identifying high-value targets for precision strikes. By leveraging the intelligence gathered through a combination of traditional and technological means, the U.S. military was able to effectively neutralize enemy threats and disrupt their command and control structure.

As a result of their successful implementation, precision-guided munitions and targeting systems have emerged as game-changers in modern warfare. The lessons learned from their deployment in Operation Anaconda have significant strategic implications for future military operations in Afghanistan. The effectiveness and efficiency of these systems highlight the importance of continued investment in advanced weaponry and technology, as well as the integration of local forces and intelligence gathering techniques.

In conclusion, precision-guided munitions and targeting systems played a crucial role in the success of Operation Anaconda. The utilization of these advanced technologies, in combination with intelligence gathering techniques and the collaboration with local Afghan militias, proved instrumental in achieving the mission's objectives. The strategic implications and lessons learned from the operation underline the importance of leveraging advanced weaponry and technology, as well as the integration of local forces, in future military operations in Afghanistan. Operation Anaconda serves as a testament to the power and effectiveness of precision-guided munitions and targeting systems in modern warfare.

Advancements in Communication and Information Systems

In the modern era of warfare, communication and information systems play a crucial role in the success of military operations. The 2002 U.S.

military operation in Eastern Afghanistan, known as Operation Anaconda, witnessed significant advancements in these areas. This subchapter explores the various technological breakthroughs and strategies employed during the operation, shedding light on their impact and effectiveness.

One of the key advancements in communication systems during Operation Anaconda was the utilization of satellite-based communication tools. These tools allowed for real-time information sharing between different units, enabling commanders to make quick decisions based on accurate intelligence. This was particularly important in a complex and dynamic battlefield like Eastern Afghanistan, where the terrain and enemy movements posed significant challenges.

Furthermore, the operation saw the deployment of advanced information systems that facilitated efficient data collection and analysis. These systems integrated multiple data sources, such as aerial reconnaissance, ground-based surveillance, and intercepted communications, to provide a comprehensive situational awareness to the military commanders. This enhanced the effectiveness of intelligence gathering, enabling the identification of enemy positions, movements, and intentions.

Another notable advancement was the use of unmanned aerial vehicles (UAVs) for surveillance and reconnaissance purposes. These UAVs, equipped with high-resolution cameras and other sensors, provided real-time video feeds and intelligence, allowing for better target identification and tracking. The use of UAVs also reduced the risk to human lives, as they could be deployed in areas with high enemy activity without endangering soldiers on the ground.

In terms of communication, Operation Anaconda witnessed the deployment of advanced encrypted communication systems, ensuring secure and reliable communication channels for the military units involved. These systems protected sensitive information from being intercepted by the enemy, maintaining operational security.

Overall, the advancements in communication and information systems during Operation Anaconda significantly improved the effectiveness and efficiency of the operation. The real-time sharing of information, integration of multiple data sources, and deployment of advanced technologies enhanced the situational awareness and decision-making capabilities of the military commanders.

The lessons learned from Operation Anaconda in terms of communication and information systems have strategic implications for future military operations in Afghanistan. The success of these advancements highlights the importance of investing in and continuously improving communication and information technologies. Additionally, the integration of advanced weaponry and technology with effective communication systems is crucial for achieving operational success in complex and dynamic environments like Eastern Afghanistan.

In conclusion, Operation Anaconda witnessed significant advancements in communication and information systems, which played a vital role in the success of the operation. The use of satellite-based communication tools, advanced information systems, unmanned aerial vehicles, and encrypted communication systems significantly enhanced the situational awareness, intelligence gathering, and decision-making capabilities of the military commanders. The strategic implications of these advancements emphasize the need for continuous investment and improvement in communication and information technologies for future military operations in Afghanistan.

Chapter 9: Psychological Operations and Information Warfare in Operation Anaconda

Importance of Psychological Operations in Eastern Afghanistan

Psychological Operations (PSYOP) play a crucial role in military operations, and this was no different in Operation Anaconda, the 2002 U.S. military operation in Eastern Afghanistan. In this subchapter, we will delve into the significance of PSYOP in the context of Operation Anaconda, examining its impact on both the local Afghan population and the overall success of the mission.

Operation Anaconda aimed to eliminate Taliban and Al-Qaeda forces from the Shah-i-Kot Valley, a rugged and hostile region in Eastern Afghanistan. To achieve this, the U.S. military recognized the importance of winning the hearts and minds of the local population. PSYOP became an invaluable tool in achieving this objective.

One of the primary goals of PSYOP in Operation Anaconda was to influence the perception of the Afghan populace towards coalition forces. By disseminating accurate and targeted information, PSYOP sought to counter Taliban propaganda and highlight the benefits of supporting the coalition. This was critical in gaining the trust and cooperation of local Afghan militias, who played a vital role in supporting the operation.

Furthermore, PSYOP helped to shape the psychological battlefield by undermining the morale and confidence of the enemy. Through the use of loudspeakers, leaflets, and other media, PSYOP aimed to disrupt enemy communication, spread uncertainty, and instill fear among Taliban and Al-Qaeda fighters. By sowing doubt and discord, PSYOP weakened the enemy's resolve and cohesion, making them more susceptible to military pressure.

Additionally, PSYOP played a crucial role in intelligence gathering during Operation Anaconda. By utilizing psychological techniques, such as deception and manipulation, PSYOP operators were able to extract critical information from captured enemy combatants. This intelligence proved invaluable in identifying enemy positions, intentions, and weaknesses, contributing to the success of the overall mission.

In conclusion, psychological operations were of paramount importance in Operation Anaconda. They not only influenced the perception of the local Afghan population but also played a critical role in shaping the psychological battlefield and gathering intelligence. By employing accurate information, strategic messaging, and psychological techniques, PSYOP operators were able to contribute significantly to the success of the mission. The lessons learned from Operation Anaconda demonstrate the vital role of PSYOP in future military operations in Afghanistan, highlighting its potential to sway public opinion, weaken the enemy, and gather critical intelligence.

Strategies and Techniques Used in Psychological Operations

Psychological operations (PSYOP) and information warfare played a vital role in the success of Operation Anaconda, the 2002 U.S. military operation in eastern Afghanistan. This subchapter delves into the strategies and techniques employed during this operation, shedding light on how psychological operations became a critical tool in achieving mission objectives.

PSYOP is defined as the use of psychological influence to shape the perceptions, attitudes, and behaviors of target audiences. In Operation Anaconda, PSYOP tactics were employed to undermine the morale and will of the enemy forces, enhancing the overall effectiveness of the military campaign.

One key strategy utilized was the dissemination of propaganda leaflets. These leaflets contained messages tailored to the specific target audience, which included both the local Afghan population and the enemy combatants. The leaflets aimed to erode support for the enemy, encourage defections, and provide reassurance to the local population about the U.S. military's intentions.

Another technique employed was the use of loudspeaker broadcasts. Special forces operators and PSYOP teams utilized loudspeakers to amplify their messages, reaching a wider audience. These broadcasts included warnings to the enemy, calls for surrender, and information about the ongoing operation. By leveraging the power of sound and voice, the U.S. military sought to disrupt the enemy's decision-making process and create confusion among their ranks.

Furthermore, the integration of social media and digital platforms proved instrumental in conducting information warfare. The military leveraged online platforms to disseminate messages, counter enemy narratives, and engage with the target audience directly. This approach allowed for real-time communication and ensured that accurate information reached the intended recipients promptly.

The effectiveness of these psychological operations was measured through continuous assessment and evaluation. Data on the impact of messages, feedback from the local population, and intelligence reports were analyzed to refine and adapt the strategies as the operation progressed.

Operation Anaconda demonstrated that psychological operations are a powerful tool in modern warfare. By understanding the target audience, tailoring messages, and utilizing various communication channels, the U.S. military was able to achieve its objectives more effectively.

This subchapter will provide historians and specialists in Operation Anaconda with a comprehensive understanding of the strategies and techniques employed in psychological operations during the operation. By examining the impact and lessons learned from these efforts, future military operations in Afghanistan can benefit from a more informed and strategic approach to psychological operations.

Role of Information Warfare in Shaping the Narrative of Operation Anaconda

In the book "Operation Anaconda: The Untold Story of the 2002 U.S. Military Operation in Eastern Afghanistan," it is crucial to delve into the role of information warfare in shaping the narrative of this significant military operation. Understanding the impact of information warfare is essential for historians studying Operation Anaconda, as it sheds light on the strategies employed to influence public perception, disseminate information, and control the narrative.

During Operation Anaconda, information warfare played a pivotal role in shaping the perception of the operation both domestically and internationally. The U.S. military understood the importance of controlling the narrative and utilized various techniques to achieve this. One such technique was the dissemination of carefully crafted press releases and briefings that highlighted the successes of the operation, downplayed any setbacks, and portrayed the military in a favorable light. This information was then shared with the media, which played a vital role in shaping public opinion.

Additionally, psychological operations (PSYOPs) were employed to influence the mindset of both the enemy and the local Afghan population. Through leaflet drops, loudspeaker broadcasts, and other means, the U.S. military aimed to erode the morale of the enemy while gaining the support of the local population. These psychological operations were designed to weaken the resolve of the enemy and create a sense of trust and cooperation among the local Afghan militias.

Furthermore, information warfare also involved leveraging technology and advanced weaponry to gather intelligence and disseminate information. The use of drones and other surveillance technology provided real-time information on enemy movements, which was then used to shape the narrative of the operation. This technological advantage gave the U.S. military an upper hand in gathering accurate intelligence and countering any misinformation spread by the enemy.

The role of information warfare in shaping the narrative of Operation Anaconda cannot be overstated. It not only influenced public perception but also impacted the success of the operation itself. By controlling the narrative, the U.S. military was able to maintain support for the operation both domestically and internationally.

For future military operations in Afghanistan, the lessons learned from Operation Anaconda regarding information warfare are crucial. Understanding the power of information and its ability to shape public opinion and control the narrative is essential for strategizing future operations effectively. By employing information warfare techniques, future military operations can aim to gain support, erode enemy morale, and shape the perception of the operation to achieve their objectives.

In conclusion, the role of information warfare in shaping the narrative of Operation Anaconda was instrumental. Through carefully crafted press releases, psychological operations, the use of advanced technology, and leveraging media, the U.S. military successfully controlled the narrative of the operation. Historians studying Operation Anaconda must recognize the significance of information warfare in understanding the operation's overall impact, strategic implications, and lessons learned for future military operations in Afghanistan.

Chapter 10: Humanitarian Assistance Efforts during Operation Anaconda

Importance of Humanitarian Assistance in Combat Operations

Humanitarian assistance plays a crucial role in combat operations, as it not only helps alleviate the suffering of civilians caught in the crossfire but also contributes to the overall success of military campaigns. This subchapter explores the significance of humanitarian assistance in Operation Anaconda, the 2002 U.S. military operation in Eastern Afghanistan.

During Operation Anaconda, the U.S. military recognized the importance of providing humanitarian aid to the local Afghan population. This approach aimed to win the hearts and minds of the Afghan people, gaining their trust and cooperation. By demonstrating care and support for the civilians affected by the conflict, the U.S. military aimed to weaken the influence of the Taliban and other insurgent groups.

One of the primary objectives of humanitarian assistance in combat operations is to mitigate the impact of conflict on civilians. In Operation Anaconda, medical evacuation and field hospital operations played a vital role in saving lives and providing medical care to those injured in the fighting. This not only helped the Afghan people but also showcased the U.S. military's commitment to protecting innocent lives.

Additionally, the provision of basic necessities such as food, water, and shelter to displaced civilians is crucial in combat operations. By addressing the immediate needs of the affected population, the U.S. military aimed to prevent further humanitarian crises and create a sense of stability in the region.

Furthermore, humanitarian assistance can serve as a powerful tool for information warfare and psychological operations. By showing compassion and care for the local population, the U.S. military aimed to counter the propaganda of insurgent groups and win the support of the Afghan people. This approach helped undermine the influence of the Taliban and other extremist organizations, ultimately contributing to the success of Operation Anaconda.

The lessons learned from Operation Anaconda and the strategic implications for future military operations in Afghanistan are significant. The effective use of humanitarian assistance in combat operations can help build sustainable peace, win the support of local populations, and weaken the influence of insurgent groups. Understanding and incorporating humanitarian assistance into military strategies is essential for achieving long-term stability and success in conflict zones.

In conclusion, humanitarian assistance is of utmost importance in combat operations. Operation Anaconda demonstrated the significance of providing medical care, basic necessities, and support to civilians affected by conflict. By employing humanitarian assistance strategies, the U.S. military aimed to win the hearts and minds of the Afghan people, weaken insurgent groups, and pave the way for long-term stability in Eastern Afghanistan. The lessons learned from Operation Anaconda can inform future military operations, emphasizing the importance of integrating humanitarian assistance into combat strategies.

Provision of Medical Aid, Food, and Supplies to Local Afghan Population

Operation Anaconda, the 2002 U.S. military operation in Eastern Afghanistan, was not only a combat mission but also an opportunity for the United States to provide much-needed humanitarian assistance to the local Afghan population. Amidst the chaos and violence of the operation, efforts were made to ensure that medical aid, food, and supplies reached those in need.

One of the key priorities during Operation Anaconda was to establish medical evacuation and field hospital operations. Special forces and medical personnel worked tirelessly to treat wounded soldiers and civilians, providing emergency care and stabilizing patients before evacuating them to more advanced medical facilities. This crucial aspect of the operation saved countless lives and demonstrated the commitment of the U.S. military to the Afghan people.

In addition to medical aid, the provision of food and supplies was vital to support the local population affected by the conflict. Humanitarian assistance efforts were implemented to distribute essential items such as food, water, blankets, and hygiene kits. These efforts aimed to alleviate the suffering of civilians caught in the crossfire and to build trust between the U.S. military and the Afghan people.

The command and control structure in Operation Anaconda played a crucial role in coordinating these humanitarian efforts. Clear lines of communication and coordination between military units, special forces, and humanitarian organizations ensured that aid was effectively delivered to those in need. This integrated approach not only strengthened the military operation but also demonstrated the U.S. commitment to upholding humanitarian principles in the midst of conflict.

Lessons learned from Operation Anaconda have significant strategic implications for future military operations in Afghanistan. The success of the provision of medical aid, food, and supplies highlights the importance of incorporating humanitarian assistance efforts into military missions. It underscores the need for comprehensive planning, coordination, and a strong command and control structure to ensure the effective delivery of aid.

Furthermore, Operation Anaconda showcased the value of local Afghan militias in supporting military operations and providing assistance to their own communities. The cooperation between U.S. forces and these militias proved to be instrumental in reaching remote areas and delivering aid to vulnerable populations.

In conclusion, the provision of medical aid, food, and supplies to the local Afghan population was a critical component of Operation Anaconda. This aspect of the operation demonstrated the U.S. military's commitment to the Afghan people, strengthened relationships with local communities, and provided vital humanitarian assistance amidst the conflict. The lessons learned from this operation have far-reaching implications for future military operations in Afghanistan, emphasizing the importance of incorporating humanitarian efforts into military strategies and the value of local support in achieving mission objectives.

Challenges and Limitations of Humanitarian Assistance in a Combat Zone

Providing humanitarian assistance in a combat zone is a complex and challenging endeavor. Operation Anaconda, the 2002 U.S. military operation in Eastern Afghanistan, faced numerous obstacles in delivering aid to the local population amidst ongoing conflict. Understanding these challenges and limitations is crucial for historians and specialists studying this operation and its implications for future military operations in Afghanistan.

One of the primary challenges was ensuring the safety and security of humanitarian aid workers. Combat zones are inherently volatile, and the presence of armed groups often puts aid workers at risk. In Operation Anaconda, the U.S. military had to develop strategies to protect humanitarian personnel, such as establishing secure zones and coordinating with local Afghan militias for their safety.

Another limitation was the difficulty of accessing remote and isolated areas where aid was most needed. Combat zones are often characterized by rugged terrain and limited infrastructure, making it challenging to reach affected communities. The U.S. military had to rely on specialized air support strategies, including helicopters and unmanned aerial vehicles, to overcome these geographical constraints and deliver aid efficiently.

Intelligence gathering techniques were also critical in determining the areas most in need of humanitarian assistance. However, gathering accurate and timely intelligence in a combat zone is inherently challenging. The presence of enemy forces, the fluidity of the situation, and the need to balance military objectives with humanitarian efforts complicated the intelligence-gathering process during Operation Anaconda.

Furthermore, the coordination and collaboration between local Afghan militias and international forces was essential for the success of humanitarian assistance efforts. Local militias played a crucial role in supporting Operation Anaconda by providing intelligence, security, and logistical support. However, challenges arose in effectively integrating these militias into the overall command and control structure, which required careful navigation.

Additionally, the provision of medical evacuation and field hospital operations faced significant challenges in a combat zone. The risk of casualties and the need for rapid medical response necessitated the establishment of well-equipped field hospitals and efficient evacuation processes. However, the ever-present threat of enemy attacks and the scarcity of resources in remote areas hampered these efforts.

Despite these challenges and limitations, Operation Anaconda demonstrated the use of advanced weaponry and technology in supporting humanitarian assistance. The U.S. military employed state-of-the-art equipment, such as drones for reconnaissance and surveillance, to enhance the effectiveness of aid delivery.

Psycho-social operations and information warfare also played a significant role in Operation Anaconda. The military employed psychological operations to shape the narrative and gain the support of local communities, highlighting the importance of winning hearts and minds in a combat zone.

In conclusion, the challenges and limitations of providing humanitarian assistance in a combat zone were numerous during Operation Anaconda. However, innovative strategies, collaboration with local militias, advanced technology, and psychological operations enabled the U.S. military to overcome many of these obstacles. Understanding these challenges and their implications is crucial for historians and specialists studying the operation and formulating strategies for future military operations in Afghanistan.

Chapter 11: Lessons Learned and Strategic Implications of Operation Anaconda for Future Military Operations in Afghanistan

Analysis of the Successes and Failures of Operation Anaconda

Operation Anaconda was a significant military operation conducted by the U.S. forces in Eastern Afghanistan in 2002. This subchapter aims to provide a comprehensive analysis of the successes and failures of this operation, examining various aspects such as special forces operations, air support strategies, intelligence gathering techniques, and more. This analysis is intended for historians and individuals interested in understanding the intricacies of Operation Anaconda and its implications for future military operations in Afghanistan.

One of the notable successes of Operation Anaconda was the effective utilization of special forces operations. The operation involved highly trained and skilled Special Forces units, who played a crucial role in gathering intelligence, conducting reconnaissance, and engaging enemy forces. Their expertise and ability to operate in hostile terrain significantly contributed to the success of the operation.

Another success was the strategic employment of air support strategies. The U.S. forces demonstrated the effective use of close air support, aerial reconnaissance, and precision airstrikes. These air assets provided crucial support to ground forces, helping to neutralize enemy positions and disrupt their command and control.

Intelligence gathering techniques employed during Operation Anaconda also played a critical role in its success. The integration of human intelligence, signals intelligence, and imagery intelligence provided commanders with valuable insights into enemy activities and intentions. This intelligence fusion enabled effective planning and execution of operations.

The role of local Afghan militias in supporting Operation Anaconda was also a success. These militias, with their knowledge of the local terrain and culture, proved to be valuable assets in gathering intelligence and conducting operations. Their cooperation and assistance in securing the area and identifying enemy positions greatly contributed to the overall success of the operation.

However, Operation Anaconda also had its share of failures. The analysis of the command and control structure revealed several shortcomings, including coordination challenges and communication issues between different units. These weaknesses hindered the seamless execution of operations and resulted in missed opportunities.

Additionally, while the use of advanced weaponry and technology was a success, there were instances where the enemy adapted to these advancements, resulting in unexpected challenges for the U.S. forces. The need to continuously innovate and stay ahead of the enemy's capabilities became evident during the operation.

Furthermore, psychological operations and information warfare during Operation Anaconda were not as effective as desired. The analysis indicates that more targeted and strategic efforts could have been made to influence the local population and gain their support.

Despite these failures, Operation Anaconda also witnessed successful humanitarian assistance efforts. The provision of medical evacuation and field hospital operations played a crucial role in saving lives and fostering goodwill among the local population.

In conclusion, the analysis of the successes and failures of Operation Anaconda provides valuable insights for historians and individuals interested in understanding the intricacies of this military operation. It highlights the importance of effective special forces operations, air support strategies, intelligence gathering techniques, and the role of local Afghan militias. Furthermore, it emphasizes the need for a robust command and control structure, continuous innovation, and targeted psychological operations in future military operations in Afghanistan.

Tactical and Strategic Lessons Learned from Eastern Afghanistan

Introduction:

In the subchapter titled "Tactical and Strategic Lessons Learned from Eastern Afghanistan," we delve into the comprehensive analysis of Operation Anaconda, the 2002 U.S. military operation in Eastern Afghanistan. This content focuses on providing valuable insights and lessons for historians and niche audiences interested in various aspects of the operation, including special forces operations, air support strategies, intelligence gathering techniques, local Afghan militias, medical evacuation, command and control structure, advanced weaponry and technology, psychological operations, humanitarian assistance efforts, and the strategic implications of Operation Anaconda for future military operations in Afghanistan.

Lessons Learned:

1. Special Forces Operations: Operation Anaconda witnessed the exceptional performance of Special Forces in conducting covert operations, gathering intelligence, and executing precision strikes. Their adaptability and ability to integrate with local Afghan militias proved instrumental in achieving operational success.

2. Air Support Strategies: The operation highlighted the importance of close air support and the effective coordination between ground forces and air assets. The utilization of advanced aerial platforms and the

integration of unmanned aerial vehicles (UAVs) enabled precise strikes, enhanced situational awareness, and minimized collateral damage.

3. Intelligence Gathering Techniques: Operation Anaconda showcased the significance of diverse intelligence sources, including human intelligence (HUMINT), signals intelligence (SIGINT), and open-source intelligence (OSINT). The fusion of these sources facilitated the understanding of enemy capabilities, intentions, and vulnerabilities.

4. Role of Local Afghan Militias: The engagement and support of local Afghan militias proved crucial in gaining local knowledge, providing cultural insights, and augmenting the operational capabilities of U.S. forces. Building trust and forging partnerships with these militias contributed to successful counterinsurgency efforts.

5. Medical Evacuation and Field Hospital Operations: Operation Anaconda highlighted the importance of efficient medical evacuation capabilities and the establishment of field hospitals near the battlefield. Rapid medical response, well-coordinated evacuation plans, and skilled medical personnel played a critical role in saving lives and maintaining the morale of the troops.

6. Command and Control Structure: Analysis of the command and control structure revealed the need for decentralized decision-making, effective communication, and seamless coordination between different units and branches of the military. Flexibility, adaptability, and clear lines of authority were vital in ensuring mission success.

7. Use of Advanced Weaponry and Technology: Operation Anaconda showcased the efficacy of advanced weaponry and technology, including precision-guided munitions, night vision devices, and surveillance systems. These capabilities enhanced the operational reach, accuracy, and survivability of U.S. forces.

8. Psychological Operations and Information Warfare: The integration of psychological operations and information warfare played a significant role in shaping the information environment, countering enemy propaganda, and influencing the local population. Effective messaging and narrative control were crucial in gaining support and undermining the enemy's influence.

9. Humanitarian Assistance Efforts: Operation Anaconda highlighted the importance of conducting humanitarian assistance efforts alongside military operations. These efforts helped build relationships with local communities, gain trust, and create a positive perception of U.S. forces.

10. Lessons Learned and Strategic Implications: Operation Anaconda provided valuable lessons and insights for future military operations in Afghanistan. These include the need for a comprehensive understanding of the local dynamics, the importance of integrating local forces, the significance of intelligence fusion, the utilization of advanced technology, and the emphasis on winning hearts and minds.

Conclusion:

The subchapter on "Tactical and Strategic Lessons Learned from Eastern Afghanistan" provides a comprehensive analysis of Operation Anaconda, highlighting the various aspects of the operation and their implications. This content serves as a valuable resource for historians and niche audiences interested in understanding the intricacies of the operation and drawing insights for future military endeavors in Afghanistan.

Implications for Future Military Operations and Counterinsurgency Strategies in Afghanistan

The 2002 U.S. Military Operation in Eastern Afghanistan, also known as Operation Anaconda, has left a profound impact on the landscape of future military operations and counterinsurgency strategies in Afghanistan. This subchapter aims to delve into the various implications that emerged from this significant operation, providing valuable insights for historians, as well as the niches interested in the different aspects of Operation Anaconda.

One of the key takeaways from Operation Anaconda is the crucial role played by special forces operations. The operation highlighted the effectiveness of these highly trained and specialized units in executing vital missions, including reconnaissance, target acquisition, and direct action. The success of these special forces units in Operation Anaconda underscored the importance of their continued involvement in future military operations in Afghanistan.

Furthermore, the operation shed light on the innovative air support strategies employed during the mission. The integration of helicopters, gunships, and close air support played a pivotal role in providing crucial firepower, reconnaissance, and logistical support to ground forces. The lessons learned from these air support strategies can be applied to future operations, emphasizing the need for close coordination and effective communication between air assets and ground forces.

Intelligence gathering techniques were also critical during Operation Anaconda. The operation witnessed the utilization of advanced technology and human intelligence networks to collect and analyze information, enabling the coalition forces to identify insurgent strongholds and disrupt their operations. The successful implementation of these intelligence gathering techniques offers valuable insights for future military operations in Afghanistan, emphasizing the significance of investing in intelligence capabilities.

Additionally, the role of local Afghan militias in supporting Operation Anaconda cannot be understated. These militias provided vital support to coalition forces, assisting with intelligence gathering, securing key areas, and engaging with the local population. Understanding the dynamics of these local militias and harnessing their support can serve as a valuable asset in future counterinsurgency efforts in Afghanistan.

The medical evacuation and field hospital operations during Operation Anaconda demonstrated the importance of having robust medical support capabilities on the battlefield. The ability to rapidly evacuate and treat wounded personnel greatly contributed to the overall operational success and can serve as a blueprint for future military operations in providing quality healthcare in hostile environments.

The command and control structure in Operation Anaconda showcased the importance of effective leadership and coordination among various military units. The success of the operation can be attributed, in part, to the clear lines of communication and the seamless integration of different branches and units. Future operations can benefit from studying this command and control structure, emphasizing the need for efficient coordination and unity of effort.

The use of advanced weaponry and technology in Operation Anaconda highlighted the significant advantages they offer on the modern battlefield. The operation showcased the effectiveness of precision-guided munitions, unmanned aerial vehicles, and other advanced systems. The lessons learned from their successful integration can inform future military operations, emphasizing the importance of investing in cutting-edge technology.

Psychological operations and information warfare also played a crucial role in Operation Anaconda. The operation demonstrated the effectiveness of disseminating accurate information, countering enemy propaganda, and winning the hearts and minds of the local population. Future military operations can learn from these psychological operations, recognizing the importance of shaping the information environment and leveraging it to gain support and undermine the insurgency.

Furthermore, Operation Anaconda highlighted the significance of humanitarian assistance efforts. The operation witnessed the provision of medical care, food, and other essential aid to the local population, fostering goodwill and strengthening the bond between coalition forces and the Afghan people. This emphasis on humanitarian assistance can serve as a model for future military operations, underscoring the importance of winning the support of the local population through tangible actions.

Lastly, Operation Anaconda provided a wealth of lessons learned and strategic implications for future military operations in Afghanistan. These lessons include the importance of adaptive and flexible strategies, the need for sustained commitment and resources, and the necessity of fostering strong partnerships with local forces and international allies. Understanding and implementing these strategic implications can significantly enhance the effectiveness of future military operations in Afghanistan.

In conclusion, Operation Anaconda has left a lasting impact on future military operations and counterinsurgency strategies in Afghanistan. From the role of special forces operations and air support strategies to intelligence gathering techniques and the use of advanced weaponry, this operation has provided invaluable lessons for historians and niche audiences interested in various aspects of Operation Anaconda. By analyzing these implications, future military operations can be better prepared to navigate the complex challenges of Afghanistan and achieve their objectives effectively.